# TELEVISION
## IS THE NEW
# TELEVISION

# TELEVISION
## IS THE NEW
# TELEVISION

## THE UNEXPECTED TRIUMPH OF
## OLD MEDIA IN THE DIGITAL AGE

# MICHAEL WOLFF

PORTFOLIO / PENGUIN

PORTFOLIO / PENGUIN
An imprint of Penguin Random House LLC
375 Hudson Street
New York, New York 10014
penguin.com

ISBN 978-1-59184-813-4

Printed in the United States of America
1   3   5   7   9   10   8   6   4   2

Set in ITC Giovanni Std
Designed by Alissa Rose Theodor

# CONTENTS

# TELEVISION
## IS THE NEW
# TELEVISION

# PROLOGUE

## THE STORY. THE MUSIC. THE LAUGHS.

On November 14, 2007, Kevin Morris, a forty-four-year-old enter-tainment lawyer, given to penumbral debates about modern culture and the state of media, and with a roster of major Hollywood clients, convened a daylong meeting in his law firm's Los Angeles offices in the Creative Artists Agency building on the Avenue of the Stars.

A year after Google bought YouTube, Morris was wrestling with the increasingly fraught relationship between the traditional media business, which almost all of his clients were part of, and the new, aggressive posture of digital media, located 350 miles north, and a world away, in Silicon Valley. Morris, aware as everybody was of what had happened to the music industry, saw this as something of an emergency moment.

At the same time, Morris felt that logically both sides had a set of common interests, and in the end certainly needed a working understanding.

His collegial idea was to assemble interested players on both sides to discuss this shared ground, because, as he said optimistically in his invitation: "It's about the story. It's about the music. It's about the laughs."

On the old media side, you had Brad Grey, the chairman of Paramount Pictures and producer of *The Sopranos*; Doug Herzog, who had variously run Comedy Central, MTV, and Fox Television; Kevin Reilly, a senior executive at NBC and Fox; Anthony Zuiker, the creator of *CSI*; Matt Stone, the cocreator and coproducer of *South Park*; LL Cool J, the actor and rapper; Michael Mann, the film director; Donny Deutsch, the advertising executive and CNBC personality; and Scarlett Johansson, John Cusack, and Matthew McConaughey, the actors.

No matter how successful—perhaps as a particular result of their success—each reflected the anxieties of an industry that was ever more frequently being told it was threatened on all fronts and, culturally speaking, totally yesterday.

On the digital side, you had a less august but significantly more cocky group: Jordon Hoffner of YouTube; Kurt Abrahamsen and Adam Stewart from Google in Los Angeles (the home office had passed on the invitation); Mark Kvamme of the venture capital firm Sequoia Capital, which had backed the Web series *Funny or Die*; and Marc Andreessen, the creator of Netscape, on his way to being among the most significant and influential venture capital figures in Silicon Valley

The imbalance was notable and uncomfortable for everyone—

or at least for everyone on the old media side. There was, even, a kind of slack-jawed response—perhaps not least of all because Hollywood power is not used to being challenged—to the certainty, impatience, and what rather seemed like the advanced intelligence of the tech side. Very quickly it all seemed something like a math class mixing slow students with advanced ones.

Morris began the day gamely recalling his college economics and Joseph Schumpeter and creative destruction and the need to come to terms with how great transformations happen—how to manage destruction. He drew a triangle on a whiteboard, with one point for tech, one point for talent, one point for media companies. We are all in this together, he said confidently.

When that did not get an obvious assent, he changed it into a kind of exhortation: "Are we all in this together?"

"Well, that depends," responded Andreessen finally.

The technology view was in fact quite the opposite of dependence or cooperation or much meeting of the minds. It was rather that the new digital media world had unlocked media secrets: user-generated content, and new types of functionality, and a view of media that embraced remarkable new efficiency and could now only look at the traditional media discipline as hopelessly inefficient.

Kvamme, sure that *Funny or Die* would trump in its over-the-top distribution and bare-bones economics the $2-million-an-episode *South Park* with its cumbersome and costly Viacom–Comedy Central relationship (the *South Park* creators had just negotiated a 50/50 deal to split digital profits with Viacom, which had committed to handling advertising), got up and went to the whiteboard and brusquely erased "media companies" on the triangle, replacing it with just "consumer"—emphasizing this new, disintermediated world.

The Google guys were even more direct, pointing out, with some impatience, that there was quite some lack of understanding in the room about the nature of the revolution that was under way.

It was Andreessen, whose word alone would come nearly to have the power to create tech success, who was perhaps most daunting and in the end most frightening—signaling how far apart the two sides were, and how precarious the television business suddenly seemed. Andreessen's lack of regard seemed all the more confounding because he kept expressing his own personal enthusiasm for television, telling everyone what was on his list to watch in the coming weeks. And yet that sentiment was divorced from the future as he saw it and as he described the complicated new terms and relationships in a world of digital media.

Finally, to what had become from Morris a kind of plea—"Are we in this together?"—Andreessen replied, "Excuse me. We are against each other. This is a zero-sum game."

"We all wanted to run away," recalled Matt Stone in 2014.

A funny thing happened over the intervening years, though. A strange schism developed. While everywhere there was the belief, near absolute, that the future of media lay with some ever-transforming technology, twenty years into this revolution, the value of traditional media, even with big losses in print and music, dramatically grew, with an Ernst & Young study in 2014 finding traditional media and entertainment companies increasing "their lead as one of the most profitable industries," with television margins as high as almost 50 percent.

And yet, at the same time, there was the unquestioned certainty that technology had fundamentally altered media behavior and scale—Mark Zuckerberg would say in late 2014 that you can't really build a business with fewer than a billion users—and hence the nature of media leadership and economics.

In fact, Matt Stone's *South Park*, continuing its remarkable seventeen-year run on Comedy Central, recently made a $30 million yearly digital deal with Hulu, while *Funny or Die* languished.

Despite all this, the belief continues, cultlike, that digital media will soon and decisively prevail.

# PART 1

# THE REVOLUTION IS FORETOLD

# 1

# BLINDED BY THE NEW

It's not hard to make a case for the new—and for overthrowing the old. There is, for instance, quite obviously, irresistibly really, that totem of the old media establishment, the fair-haired boy of traditionalism, CBS chairman and CEO Les Moonves, with his singular passion and talent for old-fashioned American television, no matter that it seemed otherwise consigned to the dust heap.

Moonves, preserved in amber, seemed all the more galling for not understanding, or certainly not seeming to care about, his throwback status. Moonves and people like him, self-satisfied, overpaid ($67 million in 2013 for Moonves), top-down managers, whose very existence seemed to define why things stayed the same, provided both a rationale of why things needed to change, and an aesthetic counterpoint, in his meticulous suits, to what a thinking, feeling, progressive media person wanted to be (T-shirt

and open-plan office). Moonves was Hollywood and show business, as hoary as the Borscht Belt.

Brian Roberts, the Comcast scion, was even more sinister and
harder to understand—hard at least to understand why he would
get any satisfaction from what he did, or how he could justify his
retro place in a changing world. He ran a cable company—that is,
bad technology about to be overwhelmed by new technology, dependent not on innovation but on backroom deals, not on giving
a customer as good an experience as possible, but on giving them
as mean and stingy an experience as they would tolerate.

These emperors with no clothes, their riches as ironical as
they might be yet plentiful, ran an industry that, if not yet dying,
deserved to die.

And the amount of money pouring into the new, no matter
that it was purely speculative money, seemed to provide a blin-
dingly clear argument for which side to root for.

Without proof that a new entertainment or news business,
publishing or broadcast, would or could emerge, something close
to revolutionary conviction swept through the media industry:
the new was certain and inevitable.

In many ways, this story of transformation and redemption was
enabled by the new medium itself—the ability to advocate for the
primacy of a new media was as potent a function of the new media
as the ability, at an ebullient, if illusory, moment in 2011, to argue
for a new Egypt. The new media reflected the passions and righteousness of the users of new media. In this, an entire subset of journalists, as specialized as political journalists but with an even more
pronounced and accepted bias, came into being: technology jour-

nalists whose very jobs and identity were hitched to proselytizing for technology.

Jeff Jarvis, a Time Inc. editorial bureaucrat who had helped found the magazine *Entertainment Weekly*, but had been jettisoned from the company not least of all for his intractable views (not just about new media, but about everything), emerged as a new media disciple—fierce, knowing, righteous, implacable, indefatigable, and convincing (anyway, he wouldn't stop until you gave up arguing). Kara Swisher, a former *Washington Post* journalist living in San Francisco—enmeshed in the technology business culture, including having a partner who worked as a senior Google executive—became a tech propagandist and personal power center through a column in *The Wall Street Journal* and then with a *Journal*-sponsored conference.

The hierarchical media business was, arguably, disrupted not so much by new technologies as by those lower down on the media ladder suddenly being able to push up by seeming to be more farsighted, more quick-witted, more knowing, more adventurous. The economic power might still reside with the old, but who would not choose foresight over temporary riches?

Ken Lerer, for example, Michael Milken's PR man in the 1980s, and one of the most astute media players (and, subsequently, tech players), went to AOL as its PR chief, helping to create an extraordinary public profile for the company, one that formally turned tech into media. That in turn led to Time Warner's disastrous merger with AOL, among other results, cementing the impression that technology-led media companies were a thing apart from old-fashioned entertainment and journalism media companies. After that, the prescient Lerer went on to team with Arianna Huffington, a media figure of indefatigable energy and canny opportunism, and together they built *The Huffington Post*, which, in almost no time at all, grew into one of the country's major news outlets—with an audience bigger than that of *The New York Times* and CNN. Lerer, following the sale of *The Huffington Post* to, in an ever more incestuous world, AOL, went on to start *BuzzFeed*, the next benchmark of media traffic growth, which, as an indication of old media discomfort with itself, becomes one of the main points of reference for Jeff Zucker—quite as much a television and old media character as Moonves—when he takes over CNN, announcing to the CNN staff that *BuzzFeed* is where his son gets all his news. (The teenage children of media executives became the era's go-to consultants.)

In many ways, the case for a new medium, run by new people, with new techniques and new motivations and, implicitly, a new message, became one of the major journalistic stories of the time—albeit one of insiders talking to insiders.

There was simply no argument: a vast and successful industry, based on deeply ingrained consumer behavior, long business relationships, and an entrenched power structure, was, inevitably and quickly, going to be transformed. And its leadership would be assumed by an entirely new group of people whose important credentials included little or no experience with media as it had been. This was industrial transformation on the level of buggy giving way to automobile. That kind of sweeping language and apocalyptic view helped create a consensus opinion not only among the new group, but, in short order, among much of the old group as well.

Everybody except the hoariest of the old—like Moonves—believed.

There was, notably, *The New York Times*. It began to propound a clear thesis and strategy: it would gradually relinquish its attachment to print and become a digital version of itself. That is, one of the nation's most influential media outlets, perhaps having its greatest influence among media people, had wholly bought the argument about the certainty and necessity of industrial transformation in its business and was remaking its own future around it. This, despite the fact that almost 80 percent of the company's revenue, even in 2014, continued to derive from the print version. It had given up most efforts to protect its shrinking but profitable business, in favor of a new business a fraction of the size, on the hope and dream that—even absent any such successful demonstrations of this strategy anywhere in the newspaper business—it would one day grow to a level that might support its costs. *The Guardian* in London, suddenly competing with *The New York Times* in this new profitless space (hence a new sort of competition: who could dig the deeper hole), made this something more than a perplexing business choice; it made it a moral one. Forward-thinking journalism, journalism that could express the ever more democratic inspirations of the age, was digital. (Curiously, *The Guardian*'s first foray into digital media was as *Wired* magazine's partner in a UK launch, which ended in tears because *Wired*'s founders thought the *Guardian* leadership was too stuck in the past, making the defensive *Guardian* people all the more determined to prove that they weren't!)

Fundamentally it's a generational argument, as so often happens in media. The old folks die, the young take over. Don't they? You really don't have to prove anything, other than that the old get ever older and then die (pay no attention to the fact that the young get older too).

The problem with this story is that none of it is true. The closer the new media future gets, the further away victory appears.

This is a book about what happens when the smartest people in the room decide something is inevitable, and yet it doesn't come to pass. Omens have been misread, tea leaves misinterpreted. Not only has the Web not destroyed TV, but the source of new media's strength—attracting ever more traffic, truly phenomenal traffic—may in fact become its greatest weakness.

These manifestos and venture financing rounds are based on a set of assumptions that were wrong from the start, and compounded as each year passes. The consequences of this folly are far-reaching for anyone who cares about good journalism, enjoys bingeing on Netflix, deals with advertising through their job, or plans to have a role in the future of the Internet.

What we need is a better, more honest guide to the changing media landscape, one based on a clear understanding of who makes money, and how.

## 2

# THE LOGICAL OUTCOME

Few innovations have been as unclear in what they would become and what they could offer and yet been greeted with as much certainty and enthusiasm as digital media. In fact, what media was going to become as a digital form—information and entertainment bought and packaged and delivered to an audience—happened to be, in the most cautionary terms, a lot like Yahoo.

Not only has Yahoo wrestled for the better part of two decades with how to make money, but, going to the heart of the problem, it has, trying countless strategies, failed to engage its users in a relationship that is very valuable.

Within a few years of its launch in the early 1990s, Yahoo had already lost much of its technological reason for being. Although it had won the first round of the search engine wars (or portal wars against Excite, Lycos, and others), it lost the more important showdown to Google, and, in fact, shortly hired Google to provide its central search function (now provided by Microsoft). Nor was Yahoo able to compete in the new ad network and search-word bidding systems in which Google was the leader (here, too, it tried to outsource to Google).

Still, its early dominant Web position left it, even now, as one of the five busiest sites on the Web.

The good news, it had an audience. Yahoo was an early demonstration of Web traffic as a structural condition—once the Web beats a path to your door, people keep taking it. The bad news, other than offering specific functionality (e-mail, chat, stock quotes), which other sites were doing as well or better, it had nothing to give its audience. It was quite a bad dream scenario: an audience, a stage, and only a tongue-tied techie on it.

With no products to sell, and no hope of charging for memberships or subscriptions, Yahoo had only ad revenue as a viable source of income.

Yahoo's desperate search for more eyeballs became the first leap by a technology company—an enterprise dedicated to executing specific functions—into the new notion of monetizing an audience by any means possible. Media by any other name, but in a sense even more basic. After all, most media begins with an idea, a genre, a point of view, a talent, a conceit about what an audience might find compelling. (Movies and radio began with a compelling technology, but immediately adapted it to traditional dramatic storytelling; television followed this model.) Yahoo had only an audience.

It was, therefore, in some sense a pure test kitchen. What will people eat?

Beyond basic functionality, what can the Web offer a mass

audience that will sustain interest on an ever-returning basis, and that will create an environment and relationship that advertisers will profitably pay for?

The failure to achieve something unique, something that would have ever-growing value, was not just the fault of technologists without narrative and emotional acumen. The technologists were still there, arguing for new efforts at useful functionality. But, as part of the objective test, senior-most media people were recruited to the company—again, a first for the Web—to turn Web formats into media formats (to be distinguished from media companies' trying to turn media formats into Web formats).

In 2001, Terry Semel, the former chief executive of Warner Bros., and arguably one of the most successful entertainment executives of all time, became Yahoo's CEO—commuting in his private plane, to deafening murmurs of resentment, from Los Angeles to Sunnyvale.

Semel wasn't the only commuter. More than any other native Web platform, Yahoo would become the redoubt of a wide range of media executives, some on voluntary or forced hiatus from traditional media, some looking for a way into what seemed like lucrative new media, some part of a new bureaucracy of crossover media-tech executives. At the same time, one can hardly blame the results on the limited tech skill sets of the media types, as might be the case with sites launched by magazines and newspapers with only catch-as-catch-can technical support. Yahoo was as well resourced from a technical point of view as all but a handful of Web companies. What's more, leadership in the coming years would shift back and forth between the technology and media sides—no, the talent resources were not to blame. (Of course, not surprisingly, and complicating the game, the two sides mostly hated each other.)

A reasonable conclusion was that it was the form itself—the Web as smorgasbord of entertainment, information, and functionality choices—that was troubled. Yahoo may be the most prominent example of the form, but it was imitated (or it imitated) other well-financed rivals, most notably AOL and MSN, which had even less success (and, in its next-gen iteration, *The Huffington Post* and *BuzzFeed*).

Curiously, what these large aggregating sites came to resemble is the form the digital world most derided: newspapers. Not just newspapers, but the anodyne, saccharine, supplement-weighted newspapers that would come to take over much of the middle market (most memorably mocked in *National Lampoon*'s 1978 parody *The Dacron Republican-Democrat*). The media portals offered generic wire-service news amped up by heartfelt or what-the-heck human interest stories and then section after section of advertising-driven content, such that it would be impossible for any user to actually offer a specific thought about the sensibility or identity of any of these mishmash sites. They existed only because they existed—in each case more by happenstance than by design.

But that is not to say they were failures either. In a way, it was something worse. It was, for all of these sites, a purgatory of ever-increasing traffic as a function of rising Web use and of ever-finer traffic aggregation methods (many of them having no relationship to user satisfaction or even active user choice), hence raising revenues and lowering user interest, loyalty, and value. As a brand concept, each of these heavily trafficked, aggregated sites became broad jokes, synonymous with failure and cultural detritus. And yet, given that each of the sites did continue to have the wherewithal to generate traffic, with its inherent commodity value, they continued to live, albeit embarrassingly and, arguably, uselessly.

A decade ago, Yahoo made a series of outside investments, of low-level value and interest at the time, in the Chinese e-commerce start-up Alibaba, and in Yahoo Japan (a separately traded public company created through a joint venture with Japanese tech giant SoftBank). Alibaba, a site that generates most of its revenue from selling things, not advertising, had a growing value that, by 2011, had come to pretty much equal Yahoo's share price. That is, Yahoo the site had no value (or even negative value).

At some point, too, Yahoo and the other traffic portals came in this sense of pointlessness to resemble media companies at their most hyperbolic worst—television at its emptiest—turning into parodies of hierarchical corporate pass-the-buck protect-your-ass bureaucracies. The open Web had become its opposite, with behavior, values, and levels of deadwood and phony-baloney jobs—and corporate-speak so deep and intense that outsiders doubled over in laughter—resembling nothing so much as the kind of companies that were regularly assaulted for being brain-dead in the 1980s and taken over by opportunistic raiders.

In 2012, the raider—or "activist investor"—Dan Loeb took a stake in Yahoo, and, with hardly any resistance, gained a dominant voice on the Yahoo board. Old-line software executive Carol Bartz, appointed Yahoo's chief in 2009, was dismissed in 2011 and replaced by Scott Thompson, who after Loeb accused him of fabricating details on his résumé was fired a few months later. Thompson was in turn replaced by the company's number two, Ross Levin-sohn, an advertising and media executive (Saatchi & Saatchi, HBO) who had become a leading media-tech crossover executive. Levin-sohn, as president of Fox Interactive Media and a key executive in News Corp's acquisition of Myspace, was like most other such crossover executives a long way from having found himself a clear success. Levinsohn was installed as CEO on an interim basis and most everyone, including Levinsohn, assumed he would be given the permanent job. His pitch to the Loeb-controlled board reflected his own experience in digital media: drastically downsize the business in an acknowledgment that traffic has, in essence, only a commodity value. Spending more money on it doesn't make it more valuable, therefore, with some clear logic, spend less. Trade ambition, or grandiosity, or panicked disarray, for cost effectiveness.

Unbeknownst to Levinsohn, Loeb was courting Google executive Marissa Mayer, who offered a general plan or at least possibility of returning the company to its technology roots—that is, to make it more Google-like, even though Google had long made Yahoo an irrelevant technology player.

With the company's shares buoyed by its skyrocketing Alibaba investment, and with Yahoo effectively acting as a tracking stock for Alibaba, still a private company, Mayer enjoyed a honeymoon period, ending only with the prospect of Alibaba's own public offering.

At this point, finding herself with a media product with little technological wherewithal or advantage, she became something of a deer in the headlights. Peculiarly, and as though in some weird admission of digital media's intrinsic problems, she gave an interview suggesting that magazines were significantly more effective media, with a strong connection to users, clear brand identity, and a focused purpose—and that Yahoo should be more like them.

Still, stuck with the imperative of holding and raising her yet gargantuan traffic base, she seemed to continue to pedal furiously to try to remain all things to all people with an ongoing series of banal initiatives—many of them theoretically magazine-like, or supplement-like, but in no way having the depth, skills, or style of a successful magazine. What's more, to hold the mass-market base, she was, while unable to make one successful "magazine," suddenly having to make many of them, each targeted to a different user and, more important, advertiser segment. (The entirety of Yahoo's operating revenues come from advertising, and yet at two major 2014 advertising gatherings—the Cannes Lions Festival in France in June, and Advertising Week in New York in October—Mayer's strange combination of terror and somnolence, including famously sleeping through a key meeting, became the main gossip, if not drama, of the events.) But magazines turned out to be something of another stopgap.

The premium plan was in fact television. Mayer hired network morning star and news anchor Katie Couric to become, Mayer hoped, a similar face and draw at Yahoo, without, of course, any piece of the complex attributes and casting dynamics that actually make Katie Couric Katie Couric (there is, for instance, hardly Katie Couric without her *Today Show* cohost, Matt Lauer).

Also, in 2014, Yahoo is reported by Nicholas Carlson, who wrote a book about the company, to have begun talks with Scripps Networks to buy its Food Network cable channel, and then to consider buying the $10 billion cable company and its entire collection of cable properties, including, in addition to the Food Network,

HGTV, DIY Network, Cooking Channel, Travel Channel, and Great American Country. Carlson also reports that Yahoo considered buying CNN. In early 2015, it was among the digital platforms, including Hulu and Amazon, bidding for the digital rerun rights to Seinfeld.

Yahoo is just one digital media company interested in what is hoped to be the next big turn of the traffic-chasing wheel: premium video.

# 3

# WHY DIGITAL IS SO SURE ABOUT THE FUTURE . . . THE MILLENNIALS!

*BuzzFeed*, one of the high peaks of millennial media, claimed an audience in 2013–14 greater than the Super Bowl's, but with only a scintilla of the Super Bowl's revenues. Instead of that being a crisis, a stark indicator of a valueless or hopelessly commodified audience, it suggested, in a sleight of hand, certain opportunity. It had the numbers, hence, of course, it would get the advertisers. No? The future only goes in one direction. (At the same time that *BuzzFeed* was making this argument, its editor, Ben Smith, was acknowledging that it probably wouldn't be around in three years, or would have transformed into something else.)

It's the twenty-year promise: we'll eat television's lunch because, tautologically, we are the future.

As per Marc Andreessen, it's zero-sum. Brand advertising is

not going to increase to support both television and digital media; therefore, one lives at the other's expense.

Because digital media is overwhelmingly ad supported, whereas half of television's income comes from other sources, brand advertising is a particularly pressing issue for the digital business. Television's largely imperturbable dominance ought to play against digital's argument. And yet it does not. History, we believe, is on the side of the rebels (although, in fact, that is hardly true at all, and it becomes more confusing when the rebels turn into the establishment).

The real narrative remains black and white. Over twenty years, television advertising has remained largely stable. Only a small number of big brand advertisers have moved substantial parts of their budgets into digital media, with the experience often being a negative or equivocal one. SNL Kagan, the television business monitoring group, lays out an extraordinary twenty-year upswing for television, from $2 billion in profits (inflation adjusted) to $20 billion in profits, with margins rising to 41 percent.

And yet digital media in that time has also, from a practically zero base, gathered, in addition to a virtually immeasurable audience, vast amounts of direct-response advertising, making it in real and extraordinary ways the other, parallel, medium and advertising destination.

But the failure to intersect becomes among the most defining features of the two mediums. In this, digital media has truly replaced newspapers' disposable, largely low-level content and cheap advertising, and television has remained . . . television.

Digital media's value, however, its yet unnatural multiples, is vastly greater than a collective newspaper. This is in part because it foresees some ultimate, monetizable, place for itself in the consumer funnel—some data-oriented, transactional, cash-register-moving result in which it might someday and somehow participate. But it is also because it continues to make the argument, in essence a demographic one, of an inevitable victory over television and usurpation of television advertising revenues.

A dip in television ad spending in late 2014 and a summer ratings drop was, again, a certain harbinger of . . . a shift.

It is the binary argument: a loss for one must be a stampede to the other.

As it happens, not only has that shift in fact yet to occur on a structural level, but when a shift does happen it tends not so much to be a shift as a downgrade, as high-margin brand advertising transforms into low-margin direct response. In this, television might lose, but likewise, digital media does not advance.

Analyst Michael Nathanson, part of a group of media analysts who have largely made their reputations by being available to the media as experts on media disruption—being press ready is the currency—argues otherwise.

In Nathanson's view—in an interview given to *Deadline Hollywood*, itself positioned as an old media disrupter, in late 2014—digital media is an unstoppable predator instilling fear in the television industry "that this is the beginning of the end of growth for television advertising. Over the past decade you've seen online [content providers] take market share from print. The worry is that there's not that much print market share to take any more. The next thing they're going to go after is television's share of advertising."

The debate, says Nathanson, reframing digital media's twenty-year wishful view of television, "is the speed of that decline [for TV]. It could be only 1% of market share or it could be 3%."

This is in juxtaposition to what he labels as conventional wisdom (although his own perspective represents quite the conventional view):

> *The mistake the analyst community is making is thinking that the share of TV [advertising] going to the Internet is just going to online video. What about social? What about mobile? What about more search spending? Look at the growth rates at Facebook or Twitter or Google. Or my friends at Iconic TV which has a JV with Jay-Z. They're getting branded entertainment dollars. They're not getting billions of dollars. But they're getting dollars. It's way too easy to say ads can't all be going to YouTube because Coke and Pepsi don't want to be surrounded by kids with skateboards going down staircases.*

In other words, advertisers are getting ready to put their top-dollar campaigns into social and search, an overwhelmingly direct-response environment filled with massive click fraud. And Iconic TV? Iconic TV? His friend? *Sheesh.* Iconic TV is a struggling YouTube production house.

No matter, we *know* millennial media habits are changing!

That's the argument that underpins much of marketing's new uncertainty and sophistry and goes in essence like this: millennials are different because they are the first generation to be raised with digital tools and digital media as commonplace; therefore, they will, ipso facto, behave differently. Or, to cast it in a longer-term marketing view, a new generation—as though never to join and become an older generation—is always an excuse to assume that behavior will change and that marketing dollars will have to adjust. It is rather safe to say things sometimes change a lot—even though, mostly, they don't change so much.

For sixty years, television, given massive generational, behavioral, and technological shifts, has managed to change . . . not so much (the world still sits in front of a television). And yet it is always, no matter its continued success, ubiquity, and cultural centrality, about to be swept away.

In the view of *The New York Times*'s style section:

The television has always been more than just an appliance. For decades, going back to the days when a single family on a block might have a color TV that the neighbors were invited in to watch, it has been a portal to a dreamscape, a status symbol, a trusted late-night companion.

Back in the Norman Rockwell days of one-career households and family dinners, that trusted cathode box was not only the centerpiece of most living rooms, it also served as a form of emotional glue for the family. Through it, the shared experiences—the Beatles on "Ed Sullivan," the Miracle on Ice—would define a generation.

But mention that experience to someone like Abigail McFee, a sophomore at Tufts University, and she may look at you with a gaze of penetrating puzzlement. She recently dropped by a friend's room on campus and beheld the most incongruous sight: a small television perched on a dresser.

Such is the soft hogwash of soft-trend reporting. Even to the extent that it is naming a real change (young people watch television less conventionally), it mixes up "TV" as a business model with "TV" as a distribution channel. TV the business model derives revenue from content pushed through a distribution network also called "TV." The health of the distribution channel is a vastly different issue from the health of the businesses using it.

Of all the bets to make, perhaps the least safe one—and the bet underpinning digital's hope of grabbing a meaningful piece of television's revenues—is that people will stop watching TV, even if they stop watching *the* TV.

# PART 2

# INVENTING
# NEW MEDIA

# 4

# HOW NEWS CAME TO
# WAG THE DOG

Most media is entertainment—narrative. Media, or its hold on us, has traditionally required beginning, middle, and end. The filmmaker Jean-Luc Godard, even at a pinnacle postmodernist moment of narrative rebellion, acknowledged as much, merely arguing they did not have to be in that order.

So it's created a basic confusion that so many media theorists and entrepreneurs frame media as, principally, or paradigmatically, news, with its weak, often necessarily fragmented, narrative structure, instead of seeing news, in business and audience terms, as a relative afterthought, and narrative—storytelling—as the main event.

This might be because would-be serious people find beginning-middle-end stories contrived and unserious manipulations—fictions—and news to be the truer thing, in fact reality. Other than for a brief experimental moment when fiction and nonfiction seemed to intersect in the 1960s, with literary types making forays into journalism and some forms of journalism becoming literature, fiction and nonfiction have mostly remained traditional counterpoints, and separate disciplines. Storytelling was diversion and escape; news was necessary, hard truth and a public good. Even as newspeople have seemed forced to say things like "it's all storytelling," that seemed more like lip service to commercialism than a new view of the news craft—and, in any event, there aren't all that many people in news or journalism, most of them literalists by temperament, who are actually good storytellers.

Or, it might be that news is held up as a primary media form because practically minded media people understand that news, for all its narrative drawbacks, is a cheaper way into the game. Media, with its influence and attention and all its potential money, is the goal, so get into it as you can—and news seems there for the taking. What's more, it isn't dependent on a unique talent—or on creating fickle things like hits. CNN and Fox News Channel first bootstrapped into media success by providing lower-cost news.

Or, it might be because at an ultimate level of media, of strategic business decisions about it, and perhaps particularly among people in the technology business—that is, people decidedly not in the media business—it is hardly understood that there is a fundamental distinction or choice, or, more important, relationship, between fiction and nonfiction, between news and narrative, between storytelling and holding the public's attention. Who wants to bet that such a balance, such an internal sort of algorithm, has ever crossed Mark Zuckerberg's mind?

Digital media defaulted to the belief that information was the currency: after all, the new medium could provide information faster, cheaper, and with greater individual specificity; the func-tional dream from the early Web and then in essence put into mass practice by Facebook and Twitter was a newspaper just for you. As digital media was killing newspapers, it was, in its fashion, emulating them too.

Digital media seemed especially suited to news not only be-cause of its speed, but because of the low value of news content. After all, digital media was all betting on the revenues to come; it had no revenues when it began.

A secret of news has always been economic triage. So much news was low cost or free filler stuff: news wires, stories rewritten from a competitor, publicity photos, hardly-rewritten-at-all press re-leases. Actual original content, not to mention actually good con-tent, or crafted content, the material that readers found of sure value and exemplary technique, was largely found only up the news value chain (in rich tabloid outlets as well as highbrow places), while the mean was happily undistinguished. Hence, an early and continuing advantage for Web media entrepreneurs: news is cheap.

Portal news outlets—Google News, Yahoo News, AOL, MSN—were all largely untended information feeds, white noise stuff, tick-ers. Then there was something like *Gawker*, which built a suite of vertical specialty sites, recycled news from other places, but added slightly more value with the briefest commentary and sense of per-sonality.

Mostly, digital news was a kind of information arbitrage: how cheaply can you acquire it, how many pennies more will advertis-ers pay for it?

Of course, as advertisers paid less, you had to produce more of it more cheaply. In some instances, news—with an added level of investment that usually meant you'd lose money—was coupled with an added strategy to build a brand and identity that distinguished news that was otherwise undistinguished. *The Huffington Post*, retailing the same information as everyone else, nevertheless managed, at least to some extent, to brand its commodity (not least of all by Arianna Huffington's own indefatigable efforts to promote the brand).

There are many reasons that make news, and time-sensitive information, a complicated and fragile value proposition. For one thing, its value quickly degrades. The lack of value of yesterday's news, in digital form, becomes the lack of value of news from two minutes ago (the speed of digital news undermined not only itself but traditional news as well—all news is, ever quicker, old news). For another, value depends on scarcity. If everybody knows the news, it isn't news; if the news is available everywhere, then you hardly do a useful or valuable job by repeating it. (Here, too, ubiquity undermined digital as well as traditional news.)

The things that might otherwise distinguish news—a long history of dependability, a unique authority, a strong personality, a level of exclusivity—were hard to establish overnight (or even in twenty years) in digital form—and even those virtues were not reliable profit drivers.

News, other than in a time of drama and crisis, has always been a sketchy business proposition, not so much dependent on its own value, but on the circumstance that has surrounded it. The happenstance, last-man-standing nature of a newspaper in a particular community. The entertainment supplements (puzzles, games, in addition to soft-feature sections) that make up the bulk of a newspaper. The early broadcast policy considerations that created well-funded, loss-

leader network news—and, for a time, there being only three networks at that. The development of unique, theatrical (attractive or
repellent) personalities in cable, and before that anchormen of
sonorous probity and a chatty family-style cast on morning TV. But in
and of itself, news—daily, low-value information—does not have the
effect on an audience that creates a particular, focused, stand-to-
attention, return-here experience.

Digital, given its reproducible, commodity-like aspects, has,
to date—to say the least—largely failed to provide the circum-
stances that might make news, or a news product, much or more
of a unique experience. Fox makes nearly $2 billion a year; CNN a
bit more than a billion—both with profit margins at more than 20
percent (often much more). There are few digital news outlets that
have more than $100 million in revenue, and those that do are
largely traditional news organizations, like *The New York Times*,
whose digital business has taken significantly more value from its
traditional business than it has created—and few of these new
outlets are profitable.

But even that overall shrinking in business value is not the
most damaging effect for digital media. Rather, the larger result is
to turn the most highly valued digital media sites into something
that, in the main, is rote, dull, repetitive, and of low value, a form
that doesn't warrant and cannot sustain focus, attention, identification, or what the marketing community calls engagement.

This may simply be the nature of information—or at least of
too much information. The natural impulse is to resist it, to skim
over it, or to be distracted by it. This is particularly true of the category known as "general interest," the information that's supposed
to attract a mass audience. It is the thinnest and most repetitive,

and, to hold what little attention you've garnered from this audience, you have to continue to produce more of it, inevitably thinner and more repetitive.

One digital media grail has always been to be the processor, the sorter, the medium's mediator, or arbiter—to be able to separate wheat from chaff. But this has effectively never happened, or no true authority has risen on a mass scale, in part because there is too much news to filter, and because the digital expectation is that anything less than at least a sense of all of it is somehow not taking advantage of the medium's ability to deliver everything. To the extent that aggregators work, they work because the sheer amount of the aggregated information distracts you from noticing the scant value of the pieces of it.

And yet still, this is the highest form of digital media, to use technology to accomplish some otherworldly form of what is now called, in a more or less holy fashion, curation. Pinpointing not just the information that you want, but information that is so personal and perfect for you that it is the stuff of emotional stickiness.

It is so targeted and cosseted that it doesn't need beginning, middle, end. Or technology supplies the work-around for beginning, middle, end.

In this, the Facebook News Feed, with its endless experimentation (including its secret efforts to determine which psychological prompts will cause which behavioral reactions), has become the potential solution, albeit the same ultimate dream: to create that fully personalized newspaper, with you and your friends the stars of a paper, then leavened with important news and relevant information.

This is largely the Facebook proposition—or at least the *cur-*

*rent* Facebook proposition: it can qualify and reorder that custom package in such a way that it will have a heightened impact on a pool of readers suitably attractive to advertisers. That is, algorithms can create not just an orderly information world, but one so personally compelling that information becomes a highly curated, contextualized, even dramatic experience.

And yet there seems to be the tacit understanding that information, bits and bites, however targeted, however personalized, however much a "shared" experience, is still a form that is inevitably skimmable and transient. The form itself needs upgrading.

And what will this upgrade actually be? "Mostly video," according to Zuckerberg, within five years.

# 5

# TO BE, OR NOT TO BE, COOL

Almost as soon as Andreessen's Netscape turned the Web into a widely available and easy-to-manipulate visual medium after its release in 1994, the comparison with television became commonplace.

The Web was potential mass media. But, with a little imagination, better. Actually, with infinite fractionalization it would also disrupt mass media, offering a more individualized and participatory experience than television ever could.

In fact, the Web, and the reasons for it, were anti-television: television was the great dumbing down; the Web was potentially the great and transforming smartening up—a media renaissance.

Given the febrile growth of the new medium and enthusiasm for it (reminiscent of nothing so much as the early days of . . . well, television), this anti-television would ultimately and surely kill the lowbrow, passive media experience.

By the same token, the anti-television, looking forward to a deeper, more engaged attention of the American consumer, would be able to support itself by aping and inevitably stealing television's business: advertising.

Still, major platforms like Google and Facebook—even if taking a chunk of television's business could vastly increase their own—certainly did not want to be thought of as television, with its significantly lower share price multiple and, culturally, its failure to adequately appreciate technology (in the parlance, its lack of innovation).

The value of a major platform derives from the potential value of its worldwide audience of billions of people, and the ways technology might transform its users' lives and alter their behavior—of course, taking a toll while doing so. The platforms, too, are, in this imagined future, a connective tissue, an ecosystem, a funnel (choose metaphor), through which other businesses will interact with its user base—and for those connections it, too, looks forward to taking a toll.

But meanwhile, the here-and-now business is advertising—albeit ambivalently.

Facebook, for instance, has an executive—an energetic woman named Carolyn Everson, based in New York, living with her family in the suburbs—who oversees advertising sales for the company. She is a media salesperson who can rather seem like a stranger in a strange land at Facebook. Her frequent presentations at sales meetings and industry events about the Facebook experience and the Facebook environment and the Facebook uniqueness, all in the kind of language that media companies use to sell and describe themselves, is peculiarly out of kilter with how Facebook itself, at its highest levels, describes itself and with what it seems to want to be.

Mark Zuckerberg is a technology-focused multibillionaire who believes his company offers a central piece of functionality in everybody's life. He seems at best impatient with if not contemptuous of media. From the beginning of his career and the earliest days of Facebook he has made sour pronouncements about advertising, seeing it, apparently, as a transitional revenue phase for the company. Sheryl Sandberg, the company's president, the default public presence for Zuckerberg who seemingly would rather not be publicly present, is a government and public affairs bureaucrat, more focused on Facebook's Wall Street and political brand (and, as the author of the women's empowerment book *Lean In*, her own personal brand) than on selling anything. That falls to Everson, who seems often quite caught off guard by how the company's own view of itself contradicts the message she is trying to relate.

Facebook, says Zuckerberg, with some impatience, is not "cool"—with cool having an apparent meaning involving pandering, or showing off, of having to chase fads, or of having to indulge the whims of customers (that is, media attributes), quite apart from the company's real nature as a vast inescapable parallel human system. To Zuckerberg, Facebook ought to be, and to him, apparently is, a "utility."

That is a strange designation in many respects, not least of all because there is always a much greater rationale for regulating utilities as necessary, and most often monopolistic, organizational structures of modern life. Governments have a clear interest in utilities, because they are a shared resource. In many parts of the world, utilities are not just regulated by governments, they are owned by them.

Utilities are in some sense the very opposite of media, the former necessary, the latter fanciful, transient, ephemeral—and that, no doubt, is Zuckerberg's point. It likely plays to the all-important engineer constituency at Facebook, that sense of building a permanent infrastructure, and, other than the word itself (with its regulatory and commodity connotations), perhaps to the investment community suggesting some ultimate, worldwide system of human dependence and efficiency (the growth stock version of Ma Bell).

But what of the people who are now paying the bills—the advertisers?

A utility is not only the opposite of media, but its negation.

Media demands an experience, a utility is a nonexperience; the less you are aware of it, the more successful it is.

Media is an environment, a utility is a conduit.

Media is a show, a utility is the back end.

And yet Facebook, and this is true as well at Google, and to an extent at Amazon, is filled with people whose very purpose is to extol the experience, the environment, and the show. It makes for a schizoid job, and a deeply divided sense of business self, making your money from a business you did not necessarily intend to be in, and which you hope to transcend.

But transcendence requires a fairly sophisticated and elaborate rationale, which seems to come down to, "We are not in the media business, we are in the improvement of, or the reinvention of the media business."

And that has turned out to be a cogent argument. Even if the media business, especially television, might be a good business, it is an unmistakably better position if you can convince people that you are creating a better business than the already good business.

That better business is going to be created of course through technology—through, theoretically, the extraordinary intelligence that the system can supply about the known desires and the predictable behaviors of the people using the system, which will enable a more efficient marketing relationship and, in short order, transaction.

Having done this, it might not just be advertiser fees that will be collected, but fees born of the leverage of causing the transaction, of collecting the money for the transaction, and of introducing other players into the funnel of such a transaction, enabling these third parties to collect fees upon which you, too, of course will take a further taste.

This ambition, however great, can seem to ignore, or obscure, or obviate the need to actually make media—that is, to put on a show. Both Facebook and Google have been quite militant about not being content creators, about not going down that slippery slope, and turning up their nose at what they suggest is a lower and more primitive order of economic activity.

When Yuri Milner, the Russian investor who would become the largest outside holder of Facebook stock, first looked at the company, it was this aspect that he found most compelling: Facebook, in an ultimate example of participatory media, had harnessed its users' enthusiasm so that they would put on the show, endlessly entertaining one another, costing Facebook nothing. For Milner this was a revolution in media—media without, well, media. No-cost media.

There is something of the reformers' zeal here. There is almost a puritanical streak about not spending the kind of money that content demands, and engaging in the wastefulness that content seems to require (many efforts to produce one hit), and as well a disdain or revulsion for the ego involved, and the resources that egomaniacs consume, and the ultimate hollowness and unattainability of the pursuit of cool.

Mark Zuckerberg is neither showman, nor salesman, nor attention seeker. And in a sense that is the audacity of his position, that you don't have to possess any of those elemental media attributes, but can still be in the media business.

That is the central bet, one that for a number of years quite cowed the media industry, that you didn't have to be in the media business to supplant it.

The problem, which Zuckerberg sheepishly avers, is that what is overwhelmingly most effective for building revenues at Facebook turns out to be video. Can you succeed in the video business without making actual media—without being in show business?

# PART 3

# THE NEW AUDIENCE— AND WHAT IT'S WORTH

# 6

# TRAFFIC PATTERNS

*I'll know it when I see it* used to be as good a method as any of identifying a valuable audience.

*New York* magazine, for instance, in 1985, its most profitable year, was one of the most distinctive and most imitated magazines in the country. It defined what was just coming to be known (and not yet disparagingly) as a yuppie. It helped create that sensibility (i.e., you could buy your identity). And part of that identity, in perfect commercial symbiosis, was *New York* magazine.

The three networks, each defining in their way an ultimate audience for American's must-have products, were also at their apogee in 1985.

A good media brand defined a good media audience.

And so valuable were these audiences that the imperative became lowering all barriers to building them. Network television, on its part, was wholly perplexed by and dismissive of the pay cable model. What did it get you to limit the size of your audience with a fee, when you could realize much more than that through advertising? Indeed, you could earn exponentially as your audience grew exponentially.

Magazines like *New York*—indeed, all consumer magazines—did everything possible to charge as little as possible so that, while still being officially "paid," they were in fact free. (Often with subscription promotions you could actually come out ahead by subscribing to a magazine. Even now you can get a free NFL-approved windbreaker from your favorite team when you pay $26 for a year's subscription to *Sports Illustrated*.)

Two things happened. These audiences became so valuable that almost everybody tried to inflate them both with free offers and with general sophistry. And they became so expensive that a separate discipline—the media buyer, or the media-buying *function*—grew up to measure and monitor these audiences.

Dennis Holt, part of the entrepreneur deal-making and freelance sales talent that follows the media business, something like prostitutes following armies, is often credited with starting the first media buying agency. The premise was simple: buying ad space required different skills from making ads. This became a hotly debated argument in the 1980s, and by the 1990s—Holt's own business, Western Media, had reached $5 billion in billings—had all but transformed the ad business.

As audiences became more valuable, the business of buying media became about measurement. It was about the quantification of an audience. The value was not in what you said to the audience, but in how you defined it. (The brand used to define the audience; now the buyers of audiences claimed to define them.)

Digital media saw the clear opportunity. In the most profitable media model, it would assemble an ad-supported free audience, but it would provide vastly more accurate and detailed "measurability" than traditional media ever could. In fact, it would provide absolute measurability—a precise count of viewers, their actions, their attentions (and lack thereof), and, too, their various personal data and preferences.

This, however, proved to be something of a tragic flaw. To the extent it was measurable, its behavior showed it to be ever less valuable.

It wasn't an audience, truly, it was traffic, which shortly became the live-and-die word of the medium. Not people gathered to pay attention. But people moving to and fro, taking a more often than not random path, seeing little, absorbing less (attention, that is, time on page, measured in fractions of a second). The better metaphor surely was a highway billboard slipping by at sixty miles an hour than a thirty-second spot.

This created a more and more difficult situation. If people weren't paying attention to ads, if they could avoid them, if they were clicking away from them in microseconds, if there was no structural way to make people pay attention, then their value would go down—a negative result of measurability. (On the other hand, for some technology people this was quite a positive result, or at least part of a deep ambivalence, with many techies sharing a basic *Adbusters* mind-set: suspicion, even paranoia, about the seductive appeal of traditional brand advertising long being a part of engineering culture; the inherent fakery of it offending the community in its pose as dispassionate believers in science, fact, and clean code.)

Beyond measurability, the lack of rumble, or echo, of jingles resonating in the brand consciousness of the nation, the absence of enthusiasm or even collective irritation for a commercial message, certainly wasn't making prices go up.

The prices went down. This was particularly good for cheap advertisers, abs-tightening-type advertisers, where the math of getting one sale could outweigh, however incrementally, the cost of having to pay for a thousand nonbuyers not paying attention. But it was off-putting to big-budget advertisers who were looking for prestige and singularity and emotional and cultural connection (and, of course, stroking of their own media and pop-culture egos).

The result was a clear new media math: to overcome falling ad prices you had to redouble audience growth.

The other side of measurability, of a traceable audience with definable behavior patterns, is that as well as counting it and categorizing it, you could manipulate it. You saw what stimuli it responded to. You could begin to see what stimuli the entire system responded to. In part that was the ad pitch—we know what people respond to, therefore, we can put that knowledge to the service of your product. At the same time, it was put to the service, not of selling more products (a more complex outcome), but of moving or producing more traffic (quite an easy result).

This became a key skill of digital media: traffic aggregation. Arguably, *the* key skill. And something of a black art. It was so valuable and necessary and refined an art that high masters of the trade became oracular, sought after, and with schools of imitators.

The point of the craft was to perfect your particular strategy before someone else—so your traffic numbers leapt ahead of your competition's. And then to come up with a new strategy before everybody else figured out your last one to stay ahead. As a strategy was established and more and more people figured it out, the traffic baseline rose ever higher. And so then you had to figure out something else to raise your base even more (and on and on).

In the beginning there was a pure arbitrage of simply buying traffic for less than you could sell it to an advertiser. But ad buyers getting smart to the arbitrage drove ad pricing down just as the demand for traffic went up (making traffic more expensive), so the arbitrage no longer worked. Then came an era of gaming search engines—search engine optimization. Everybody needed an SEO specialist, spawning a small industry of consultants. The skill here was in what information you put on a page to prompt Google and other search engine algorithms (though, of course, mostly Google) to put your page higher in their search rankings.

That is, whoever was searching on a particular keyword— "Maui," for instance, or "dialysis," or "organic"—would see your contribution on the subject, meager though it might be, first.

This had the additional and unintended effect of helping to change the very nature of a media brand. You didn't go to *The New York Times*, per se, you went to Google, who suggested not a source so much as a page, effectively freeing and leveling all information. It was surgical selection of information rather than information in the context of a particular source with an identity and history and sensibility that a reader or user in some particular way had a kinship with.

Merely grabbing a slice of information because of the ranking on a search engine—a ranking that had little to do with sensibility or context or usefulness (and, often, not much to do with information either)—created not only a new sense of informational disposability (reject, reject, reject, yeah, a little helpful), but a confusion about who was actually supplying the information, and, finally, a break in the relationship and understanding that advertisers have previously relied on and paid for between an information brand and its audience.

This provoked another fall in advertising rates, and another search for new ways to get more traffic to offset the fall.

SEO techniques became so successful that many media businesses came to be created out of providing the bare minimum level of information—functionally valueless in its lack of originality, sourcing, vetting, and accuracy—with a sophisticated level of search optimization. All of which, once more, discredited and lowered the value of digital media to advertisers. Still, if the optimization was advanced enough, that could compensate for the fall in advertising rates—again, traffic arbitrage.

This was, for a period, state-of-the-art digital media, only ultimately disrupted by Google's concern about falling cost per thousands, and hence, its calculated disruption of search algorithms, having a grievous effect on some of the biggest "content farm" businesses. (Shortly after Demand Media went public, for example, Google's first tweak to its algorithm in 2011 cut the traffic to Demand's schlock ehow.com by 20 percent; further tweaks in subsequent years delivered a series of hammer blows to Demand's stock.) This, in itself, dramatically identified another problem in digital media: traffic, because it flows downstream, can always be obstructed further upstream.

But the caravan moves on. Search engine optimization moved to "social strategy"—that is, an orchestrated plan, and precise processes, for appealing to (or drawing in—or tricking) Facebook's users. The founder of *BuzzFeed*, Jonah Peretti, has been open about the company's focus on social clicks coming out of an early experience seeing their SEO traffic choked off by a slight change in Google policies.

In other words, nobody owned their audience; they just owned technology and process, which could at any time be disrupted and made obsolete by Facebook and Google. (At Facebook this resulted, in essence, in killing the game Farmville, almost entirely marketed through Facebook, and hobbling Zynga, the company that owned it.)

And, too, there developed a perpetual loop of traffic exchanges, such that it might begin to seem that digital traffic was merely a small base multiplied by itself an infinite number of times. Sites exchanged traffic, or they "syndicated" their content into the context of someone else's content, or they became agents of third-party strategies to aggregate and sell and recycle traffic.

In fact, for most readers, the last time they read *New York* magazine was probably because they clicked on a sponsored link on another magazine's site. Outbrain, for instance, pays a large number of sites to carry its widgets (those small blocks of random stories you might find on a page). Sites agree to do this because Outbrain pays $1.50 to $3.50 per thousand views—higher than many advertisers pay. In turn, other sites contract with Outbrain to have their content displayed in these widgets with a link back to the site. For this, a content provider might pay as little as 1.5 cents per click and as much as 7 cents, depending on the level of exposure you want and the amount of traffic you seek. If you are willing to pay 3 cents a click, that might reliably earn you a million visits a month—7 cents might get you tens of millions or more. The only problem is that it is almost impossible to sell a click for more than that— though you might do less poorly if you dump a user into multiple page view slideshows or other force-you-to-keep-clicking formats.

You see the problem here: even using legitimate practices, you produce at best a drive-by audience, and one that costs more to get than you can make on it, which is, fundamentally, digital media economics.

What's more, you don't really own an audience. No audience is truly seeking you out. No audience is actually saying they like what you do. No audience is in the end attesting to your value. Other than through gimmicks, you, the audience aggregator and digital media destination, don't really exist. Or, to the extent that you do have a core audience, it is too small to support the business you've built off the illusion of a much larger audience.

None of this is without precedent in other media businesses focused on selling ads. During the 1980s when advertising was as plentiful for magazines as it has ever been, it became more profitable to add circulation to take advantage of advertising revenues at the expense of subscriptions. That is, circulation money came in more slowly than advertising money. Therefore, it was better to lose money on circulation and make it up and more on advertising. This meant, in effect, giving subscriptions away. This tactic had become so widespread that the 1990–91 recession, with its sudden deep drop in advertising spending, effectively realigned the magazine business, which had taken on a huge circulation cost that it suddenly had no ad dollars to support.

In other words, digital media had recreated the same circumstance that had imperiled much of traditional media, or at least print media—a low-value and insupportable audience.

# 7

# THE SELF-PROMOTERS

The traditional publishing business has three sides: editorial, circulation, and advertising. Editorial created the brand (i.e., sensibility), circulation provided the readers, and advertisers bought, in an artful mix, both the brand and the numbers (neither was particularly compelling alone).

Now, circulation has always been a suspect business, from buying or muscling your way onto newsstands or supermarket checkout counters, to dumping copies in hotel lobbies, to the parascience of direct mail, which is where most magazine subscriptions came from. The direct mail model was focused on a single number: response rate. If you sent out a million solicitations, how many people would respond? That number was usually well under 1 percent. So the entire job became how to lift that number, how to move the dial from .006 to .008. This was done with discount offers, or contests, or free merchandise. But, more economically, it was done by measuring the effectiveness of a range of stimuli—colors, type size, exclamation points, peel-off stickers, pictures of animals, or, in Time Inc.'s great leap forward, by developing a technology to individually address each direct mail recipient. This was the intersection of data and psychology. It was hardly the proudest part of the business; indeed it was scandal prone (organizations like Publishers Clearing House and other sweepstakes firms were always being singled out for egregious abuses at the intersection of data and psychology), and the focus of more and more regulation by state and federal laws.

Still, beyond the promotional flimflam, there was a product. The magazine, however aggressively or fraudulently it was marketed, still stood for something. It *was* something. You could evaluate the worth of the product.

In a certain curious way, digital media, and social media particularly—that perfect medium of data and psychology—has devolved only to a circulations strategy, for all intent and purpose eliminating an independent editorial product, and even advertising sales. The business is overwhelmingly, in many instances exclusively, focused on response rate. Marketing is no longer a separate function from editorial—the editorial is the marketing. The editorial is the confection, endlessly measured and adjusted against the real-time data, designed to increase response rates. There is a vast funnel of greater and lesser successful techniques at that sweet spot of data and psychology, all meant to make you click, like, share. The right tactics might increase your response by ten times, and hence, sustained over time, your VC valuation by ten times. Not incidentally, in the publishing business the promotions people were the lowest paid; in the digital media business this same function, now needing CS/engineering/math degrees, is the highest paid. It's the leadership job.

The problem is that, with most resources and skills directed at response rate tactics—and not at the creation of a message or sensibility—the only thing an advertiser has to buy is the number. (And, indeed, the method of advertising buying has become increasingly about efficiently buying those numbers—those eyeballs.) There is no unique thing to buy. Nobody is buying sensibility. Hence, the entire game is in producing greater numbers. That's everybody's game. Everybody gets ever better at producing an ever-higher response rate. But if everybody is better at it, then there are ever more eyeballs to sell, and, since every eyeball is just a function of data and psychology, no eyeball is meaningfully different from another. Not only do prices go down as inventory rises, but nobody has created a distinct product to actually capture or own those eyeballs. Every eyeball has to be captured again—as though for the first time.

Here's the effective business formula: increasing clicks (or likes or shares) + declining ad rates = billion-dollar valuations. Obviously that's an unsustainable proposition that everybody sees (and applies great sophistry in an effort not to acknowledge) and is trying to race ahead in some mostly terrified fashion (albeit with a veneer of cockiness) to correct.

*BuzzFeed*, *Vice*, and *Forbes* have been among the most adroit exploiters of these new promotional techniques—and all have understood the need to escape the confines of a model that ultimately resembles nothing so much as a pyramid scheme (not only do the techniques flatten but eventually the eyeballs run out).

In the instance of *BuzzFeed* and *Vice*, the effort is to use the digital promotional pyramid to build a brand and bootstrap themselves into a much more traditional television model; for *Forbes* the effort has been to use digital promotion to help distance itself from print—but, alas, without an endgame, or an endgame only into digital, this resulted in the destruction of its brand and the necessity of a fire sale.

## BuzzFeed

*BuzzFeed* grows out of *The Huffington Post*, perhaps the most successful example of a native, content-producing, general interest digital news product. Between 2010, when it was sold to AOL for $315 million, and this writing in 2015, *The Huffington Post* was the only sale of a non-video-content-producing digital media company—a pretty clear indication of a stalled market.

*The Huffington Post*, launched in 2005, was a next-generation instance of digital media, masterminded by Ken Lerer and branded with Arianna Huffington's name.

The early *Huffington Post* team included, in addition to Lerer and Huffington, Jonah Peretti and Greg Coleman. Lerer supplied the capital and management, Huffington supplied the promotional wherewithal, recruiting a sterling list of celebrities who would write (or blog) for free, Peretti supplied the traffic-generating strategy, and Coleman, with stints at Yahoo and AOL, supplied ad sales talent.

In 2010, after the sale to AOL, Huffington herself stayed, and Lerer backed Peretti in the development of *BuzzFeed*, with Coleman joining later.

The specific next-gen advance, or conceit, was to see *BuzzFeed* as truly new and endemic Web media. Huffington and attendant celebrities represented an old content idea. *BuzzFeed*, with Peretti's traffic methods, would generate just as much traffic by its ability to measure and quickly respond to what Web traffic was looking for. It didn't need brand—or numbers would create the brand. Hence, while it would become widely ridiculed for its cat videos and list features, it almost immediately began to build a large amount of traffic—mostly by its ability to game and respond to Facebook's dynamic.

This, too, became its fundamental advertising strategy: not your typical adjacency—that is, an ad next to content—but advertising material designed to function like *BuzzFeed*'s own content. But even here, this was a shift more subtle than it seemed—not so much, as critics said, an effort to blur the lines and confuse readers, but a way to rent *BuzzFeed* advertisers *BuzzFeed*'s traffic methodology. *BuzzFeed* wasn't fundamentally selling an audience; it was selling a process, a technology, a set of algorithms (in a way, not so dissimilar from Google's AdSense approach).

Then, in a reversal or advancement in strategy, it hired a news team for the 2012 presidential election, producing cogent political reporting and sometimes breaking stories—but within the confines of endless midway carnival call-outs and lowbrow attractions. In part, it was a television point: news divisions elevated lowbrow network television. News was the branding device. It also had a clear strategic purpose: traffic gaming and aggregation dominated the digital media business (in some more or less cynical fashion) until Google changed the way it ranked such sites, doing significant damage to these businesses overnight. *BuzzFeed*'s news was an effort to give it bona fides that might protect it in the next sweep of Web detritus.

*BuzzFeed* was, in a sense, less a media company than a technology play, meticulously and artfully developing a largely automated system (though, belying this, it still required several hundred people to help perform this task) to attract or divert traffic. But, in order not to be defeated or challenged or compromised by powers higher in the technology chain, in savvy fashion it was trying to wrap itself in the protection of a news company.

And, with its news operations during the 2012 campaign, *BuzzFeed* went from a largely disdained notion, a lowbrow traffic circus, to an exemplar of digital media—even though it still remained principally a lowbrow traffic circus. *BuzzFeed* became something of the standard-bearer. In early 2014, *BuzzFeed* floated rumors that Disney had offered to buy it for something less than a billion dollars—but *BuzzFeed* wanted *at least* a billion dollars (or wanted to turn rumors of almost a billion into anything remotely near a billion).

On the one hand, there was ever more traffic flowing into it via its symbiotic Facebook relationship, and a bubble-type valuation because of Web media's consensus that it was the breakthrough model. On the other hand, the reality: while it was claiming its greater-than-Super-Bowl-size audience, it was admitting to revenues of only $50 million a year.

By mid-2014, unable to complete its billion-dollar deal, the company instead took an investment of $50 million from Marc Andreessen's firm, which was said to value the company at $850 million (given the way venture capital funding works, with a host of preferences for the last-in investors, it was no doubt considerably less than this), and once again promoting it to ne plus ultra status.

Except, other than its continuing promotion, it had yet to boost itself above the revenue model of a single-title magazine. At $50 million a year, it was the size of *New York* magazine, which had a circulation of 400,000. Conversely, *BuzzFeed* also seemed to make the argument that it wasn't really media at all; it *was* a technology company, one that specialized in attracting traffic for brands—but that again returned to the value of that traffic. And then—now media again—there was *BuzzFeed*'s new argument that it was going to become an ever more aggressive content producer, announcing *BuzzFeed* Motion Pictures, that is to say, its plan to break into the television business. Video, in almost all *BuzzFeed*'s discussions about itself, seemed to represent its escape from the depressed digital gulch, with its valuation hinging on the belief that, somehow, it *would* escape.

Digital media's future was beyond digital media.

## Vice

A few weeks after the new investment in *BuzzFeed*, *Vice*, artfully leapfrogging a competitor, announced that it had raised $250 million from A&E Networks (A&E is owned by Hearst and Disney), valuing the company at $2.5 billion.

Almost immediately thereafter a tech venture firm, TCV, followed with another $250 million for another 10 percent. Time Warner was set to do a deal with *Vice* a few months before that would have valued the company at $2 billion—but *Vice*'s valuation rose faster than TW's ability to act. James Murdoch had already bought 5 percent for $70 million on behalf of 21st Century Fox and got a seat on the board; Martin Sorrell, chairman of WPP, put $25 million in; and Tom Freston, former Viacom CEO, put in his own money and signed up as one of the company's key advisers. One might be forgiven for thinking of Zero Mostel in *The Producers* selling a Broadway show many times over.

In Web propaganda terms, this was old media seeking comfort in new, but, more reasonably, it should be seen as new seeking safety in old.

*Vice* is a temperamental and elastic proposition. Launched before the Internet, it was originally a skateboard-focused magazine in Toronto. Identifying this dude-specific audience, it continued to service it with a dog's breakfast of media products (events, music, T-shirts, Web), curiously surviving by turning itself into more a demographic marketing company than a platform-specific media company.

And then it stumbled into video—and the new Final Cut Pro world where videos could be produced largely without training or capital investment.

As central to its character is its founder, Shane Smith, showman and promoter, more reminiscent of the media heyday—an only slightly more mild Jann Wenner or Hugh Hefner—than the tech age or even the more constrained modern media industry.

While *Vice* was suddenly associated with new media, its attractiveness was in part that it was recognizable as old media. Quite distinct in the Web media world, it had a strong voice and sensibility. (*Vice*, with its many fledgling music writers looking for a byline, is often and inexactly compared to *BuzzFeed*, with its ever-growing staff of engineers able to game the social media world.) Working with low budgets (it became a famous exploiter of young media workers), it produced massive amounts of content, most of which adhered to a focused taste and character.

What's more, *Vice* sold ads, extremely profitable ads. Like much of new media, it blurred the lines between ads and content, and advertising media and advertising creator (effectively acting as an ad agency for many of its advertisers). Unlike much of new media, it was able to sell its ads at a high margin. Many of its advertisers seem to somehow be induced into being merely the most passive of sponsors (often offering big consumer brands like Anheuser-Busch just modest sponsorship credit at the end of a video).

This is hardly the biggest anomaly. The ultimate disconnect was that it sold high-priced ads against a very small audience. You might attach many superlatives to *Vice*—it may be the hottest, savviest, coolest, richest, Brooklyn-est new media company on the block (*Vice*, according to Smith, is now the biggest employer in Williamsburg, the epicenter of Brooklyn-ness), but one peerless thing it does not necessarily have is a super-size audience. *Vice* makes a torrent of YouTube videos but most, according to YouTube stats, have only a limited viewership. *The New York Times*, in its coverage of *Vice*'s TCV deal, seemed both eager to believe in *Vice* and at the same time perplexed by it, quoting the company's monthly global audience claim of 150 million viewers, but, as well, comScore's more official and low-wattage number of 9.3 million unique visitors a month.

This is, it should be noted, a key media attribute, to be able to sell something other than numbers—and a new media Achilles' heel, that it is always selling numbers. Smith is selling that most profitable aspect of media, association, being part of some larger cultural framework: being cool.

Smith also, counterintuitively, launched his company into the news business—making itself a veritable Zelig of multiple international conflicts. *Vice*'s tipping-point moment may have been Dennis Rodman's *Vice*-sponsored embrace of Korean dictator Kim Jong-un, and its step into legitimacy its earnest HBO world report show. And yet this is at a moment when it has never been more difficult to monetize news programming. YouTube, peculiarly, is widely advertising *Vice* as a kind of new wave *60 Minutes*—as though this is something its audience has long missed in YouTube programming. So bizarre is the notion that *Vice*'s young male audience will watch international news that puzzled media minds can only seem to conclude it must be true—and another epochal media disruption. Instead, of course, it is a kind of mutually beneficial Web promotion. *Vice* gives YouTube the benefit of a news brand; YouTube gives *Vice* the benefit of an incredibly expensive national branding campaign (i.e., an old television strategy).

Smith's central premise, illusory or not, is that he has mastery of a certain audience, and sensibility, and zeitgeist zone—he's inserted *Vice* into the cultural consciousness. Again, there is no real-life manifestation of this, no particular set of characters, nor memorable phrases, nor hit shows that he can stand on. *Vice* is not *South Park*, with its millions of young devotees over now multiple generations, its cultural impact, and its guaranteed cash flow.

And yet *Vice* has created an identity and sensibility that people seem able to understand without actually having to experience it. This is media (and certainly media marketing).

And yet while Smith may be the avatar of the new—the quick, the cheap, the young, the cool, the digital—it turns out that his way forward is in fact television. What he wants most is a channel, a network, an offline place to call his own. The outline of his prospective deal at the beginning of the summer of 2014 with Time

Warner had TW selling CNN's Headline News Channel to *Vice* for a stake in the company (this is where the $2 billion valuation came from, which *Vice* then traded up to $2.5 billion). Now, A&E is suggesting that it will give up one of its lagging cable stations to *Vice*. And, in addition, *Vice* is launching a twenty-four-hour news channel with Rogers Communications, a Canadian cable company.

Smith seems to have cannily traversed the new to return to the old.

## *Forbes*

*Forbes* is a minor tragedy of brand and journalism. While other magazines were standing on the sidelines, *Forbes*, launched in 1917, was pursuing by the late nineties and early millennium an aggressively digital transformation.

In part, this was just the result of sheer bravura salesmanship. Before the reality of digital media was established, *Forbes* figured out that print CPMs—$30 to $60 in the case of *Forbes*—easily crossed over to the Web. In other words, it briefly looked like magazines could make the same revenue they always had but without attendant production and distribution costs. And *Forbes* became the leading example of the new world that awaited beyond print.

By the time that fantasy collapsed, largely with the dot-com crash, *Forbes*'s print business was in substantial decline too, making it all the more imperative to, in the yet-urgent formulation, figure out digital. And once again, pushed on by its sales staff, it did: it increased traffic.

In a sense, at this moment modern Internet publishing was invented—and it was invented at *Forbes*. What emerged at *Forbes* over the next few years was an aggressive new publishing model, focused on traffic aggregation and arbitrage, using the Web to promote itself—a reasonable definition of Web virility—matching low CPMs with mass usage, the model that *BuzzFeed* and *The Huffington Post* would adopt. Or, depending on your point of view, it was a shell game, in which, through a series of ever-developing stratagems, random eyeballs, most caught unaware and without particular interest in *Forbes*, were tricked or promoted into coming to the site.

Still, it was a kind of marvel of doing what you had to do to survive, to transform into . . . well, what was hardly clear. All other magazines appeared caught in the headlights, but *Forbes* seemed confidently to barrel on, showing the way.

Transformation, however, was far from salvation. Digitalmania was hardly replacing print dollars. After selling the *Forbes* plane, yacht, island in Fiji, palace in Morocco, ranch in Colorado, Fabergé eggs, and Fifth Avenue building, in 2006, a major part of the company itself was sold. The deal with Elevation Partners—an investment fund most notable for Bono being one of its partners—valued the company at about $500 million, putting $237 million into its coffers, with $100 million going directly to the Forbes family.

And then, in 2007, following the financial collapse, devastating many businesses, but perhaps none more so than print publishing, there was a radical restructuring of the editorial side. Lewis DVorkin had been an editor at the magazine who, with an investment from *Forbes*, had gone off to start a company called True/Slant—a user-created-content concept, meaning that anybody could write, and nobody got paid (at least not more than a symbolic dribble).

In 2010, *Forbes* absorbed True/Slant and DVorkin was given the primary editorial responsibility at the company, charged with creating a low-cost, high-traffic model.

While *Forbes* maintained a skeletal staff, in effect, anyone could write for it, with little vetting or oversight or alignment with the *Forbes* brand. In some sense, there was suddenly no *Forbes* brand—at least no specific, coherent meaning of it. Almost anybody—PR people promoting something, consultants looking for clients, science and pop-culture recappers, as well as oddball opinionists—could write for *Forbes* and claim to be a *Forbes* writer and to have been endorsed by *Forbes* magazine if they seemed likely to generate traffic.

DVorkin, rail thin with deep-set eyes, giving him something of a grim reaper resemblance, told *PandoDaily*, a tech news Web site, that traditional journalism was dead and hostile journalists should "get over it."

Journalists, he said, "need to understand the world is changing."

But this, in some curious sense, was inaccurate. Arguably, the changed world, the one *Forbes* now occupied, had proved to be a bleak existence, and the greater media effort, evident at *BuzzFeed* and *Vice*, was to return to the world of brand, narrative, consistency, and a more attentive audience.

In the summer of 2014, *Forbes* was sold to a Hong Kong–based company that proposed to use the *Forbes* brand, still of some note in many parts of Asia, to promote its own financial products.

# 8

# TECH MEN AS AD MEN

By the middle of the new millennium's first decade it was power-fully evident that a revolution in advertising was in progress. The clear early casualty was print. Key aspects of newspaper publishing, once selling $50 billion a year in advertising, fell away, central among them virtually all classified advertising—auto, real estate, help wanted—supplying most of a newspaper's profitability. There followed significant aspects of display ads—that is, big space, big budget—personal finance (credit cards), major retail (the e-commerce bite), lavish real estate entreaties, large portions of travel budgets, packaged goods, and the pages of weekend movie advertising. And then much of direct marketing was subsumed by the Web. (There are, in general, two kinds of advertising: brand advertising, which has to do with creating desire and building demand and long-term associations with a product, and direct marketing, which is about having you buy a specific product or service as soon as you can and is judged on its immediate return. The purest form of direct marketing is direct mail—magazine subscriptions, credit cards, life insurance. Since postage is expensive and digital communication free, this particular migration was a no-brainer.)

Something else happened to further the revolution and the destruction of print: a large portion of the advertising business converted itself from its dual emphasis on print and television to a new emphasis on digital together with television (these became competing power centers within agencies).

The accepted explanation is that agencies adapted to client demand and audience migration. But, as well, creating digital marketing strategies was much more profitable than creating traditional print or direct marketing campaigns. A print ad was, with only some reductiveness, a copywriter, an art director, and a photo shoot. Building a Web site meant programmers, designers, interface experts, project managers, social media gurus and implementers, and, more recently, native ad writers (not to mention engineers maintaining servers, and staff for responding to e-mails and curating message boards), all generating billable hours. So by the time this conversion was complete—first came stand-alone specialty digital agencies and then all agencies became fully integrated digital players—there was, practically speaking, no one left, save for newbies and career flameouts, to create print advertising, even for clients who wanted print ads. Ad agencies did television or digital. Period.

But then, confoundingly, catching virtually everyone quite unaware, and by any logic appearing to be an anomalous dip, Web ad prices started to fall—and then kept falling. Well, not everyone was unaware: companies paying for the advertising were not unsurprised at all.

Now, print advertising has traditionally been priced on the basis of the number of people who see the ad, that is, at a cost per thousand (mille)—CPM. The harder to reach and more sought after an audience, the more you could charge to reach it. The bigger the audience, the less you might charge, but, given mass market size, the more money you might make. The span in print might be as much as a near-$40 CPM for *Time* magazine, with its 1995 circulation of 4 million, and a $75 CPM for the more specialized *Fortune*, with a 1995 circulation of 750,000.

And, in fact, at a singular moment in time, when digital readers and analog readers seemed roughly equivalent, CPMs were equivalent too, leading the media industry to believe that the future held equal revenue with vastly diminished production and distribution costs (for magazines and newspapers, no printing and delivery).

But then, relatively quickly, you could begin to see the difference between traditional media with its fairly specific attention demands—television showed one show and one ad at a time, magazines and newspapers a page at a time—and a Web site, a new nonlinear world, a hodgepodge, a mess, an assault.

Digital advertising promised, at last, a way to measure the effectiveness of ads, especially if the ads directed readers to the brand's Web site. You could finally advertise your product to a million people and see how many of those million bought it. The answer was: disturbingly few.

Hence, the fall began, a fall vastly greater than just an adjustment for the lower cost basis. It was a fall of cataclysmic size—from average magazine highs of $30 to $50 per thousand to an average close to 10 percent of that (hence, in the new parlance, analog dollars to digital dimes) to an undifferentiated long-tail CPM of pennies. The fall implied, at least to anyone not in the strictest denial, that there was a qualitatively clear difference in behavior and in attention and in response between the digital audience and the traditional audience.

What's more, there was so much of this new audience and its accompanying ad space.

It was a pivotal economic breakthrough moment from the buyer's point of view. In the past, the price of media reflected a scarcity premium. The price was bid up in sought-after properties (that is, properties that could deliver a sought-after audience) because there was limited supply. Television had a fixed number of spots. Magazines and newspapers, even thick ones, had a maximum number of pages (although print, compared with television, could more easily expand, hence one reason it was generally cheaper to buy). But Web sites had unlimited space.

What's more, in the Web world, advertisers were not even limited to a given Web site audience. Rather, suddenly there was a growth business in middlemen audience aggregators called, ever eager to be associated with television, "networks." Google offered the biggest such network (DoubleClick was arguably the first Web-wide ad server—and purchased by Google), but there were myriad others, specialized to greater or lesser degrees, each with "inventory" available through the almost unlimited number of Web sites looking to make additional or marginal income from advertising sales.

It was a curious devil's bargain. In the past, the barrier to entry in the media business was that you not only had to have an audience but you had to have the wherewithal (a sales force) and the credibility (a brand) to sell that audience. Now, you didn't. Any network would take any amount of inventory you could give it—albeit for pennies on the traditional media dollar. Still, this revenue opportunity, as discounted as it might be, also fueled the ever-marching increase in inventory, further lowering prices.

This was then compounded by an additional form of ad sales called programmatic buying. The promise, and to a certain degree the reality, was that the audience that you paid *The New York Times* a premium to reach (because there was only one *New York Times* audience) could be assembled down to a demographic iota outside *The New York Times*—and at a dramatic discount. Hence, the already low CPMs at the *Times* became even lower outside of the *Times*, forcing the *Times* itself to lower its rates in order to compete with its own demographic, no longer anchored to the paper but free-floating in digital time and space.

Suddenly there were "buying desks" bidding for and selling an ever-expanding inventory.

The Web became a rare form of auction in which, by the math of unlimited supply, prices reliably went down instead of up.

In order to continue to advance, or at least not to shrink, almost every advertising-driven digital business had to turn to some form of traffic pumping.

This included a wide variety of new techniques—search engine optimization and then social network gaming and traffic loop aggregators—creating massive, even hyperbolic, traffic inflation.

The threshold scale in 2010 of approximately 10 million unique visitors per month needed to secure an RFP from a big media buying agency rose to 50 million uniques, or in some cases, 100 million by 2014.

Advertisers have long accused media of servicing distracted audiences (bathroom and fridge breaks in television, inattentive leafing through a magazine), but compared with digital, traditional media was something of a theater with a specific mind-set and focus. On the Web you had an audience that was as though in the middle of a busy street, its attention caught by sudden random movements, loud noises, screeching cars, ugly or comely passersby. The traditional media audience was there by choice more or less; this new audience was, more often than not, dazed and confused. Digital media thrived on distraction (distraction distracted users from focusing on how feeble it largely was) instead of limiting it.

And that is the positive side. The vastly more negative interpretation is that much of this audience wasn't an audience at all. In one study as much as one third of Web traffic was found to be the product of click fraud, that is, robots were the audience, many emanating from offshore servers, producing the clicks that sites were selling to advertisers (the Association of National Advertisers estimates that a quarter of digital video impressions are fraudulent). Some brands had taken to insisting on an arbitrary discount on the traffic they were buying by 50 percent or more.

And then came mobile—a sea-change shift to mobile—with its smaller screens, greater distractions (users were, literally, in the street), and another quantum drop in advertising prices.

# 9

# EXPLAINING PROGRAMMATIC ADVERTISING

Jay Sears got his first digital job in 1994. Out of college for a few years, he had been working for an old-line PR firm and then wandered into a start-up Internet company borrowing some space on the same floor with a question. He was a junior person on the Pizza Hut account and his question was about promoting pizza online. Twenty years later, Sears was one of the senior executives at the Rubicon Project, which declares itself "on a mission to automate buying and selling for the global online advertising industry."

In pleated khaki pants and blue blazer, Sears continues to look like a media salesperson from the greatest days of the business. But in a sense he has gone from someone like himself who would have once been representing the effectiveness of media—a highly focused audience on highly limited media space—to representing the ineffectiveness of it: a vastly larger, unimaginably more dispersed audience, with unlimited media space.

Sears, who might have once been the marketing face, the personal relationship at the heart of the media business—and he still maintains a salesman's bonhomie and good cheer—is now the opposite: he's a leader in a business proposing to remove the salesman from media sales.

In many ways, of course, it was the salesman, as part of a classic boys' club, who maintained the price of media. Media space held its high price because there was a limited amount of it and because a high price was good for the media that sold it and the ad agencies that received a commission on the sale when they bought it for willing brands.

But digital media turned advertising into an existential issue: there is just too much advertising space. In effect, the audience is too large. Not only is there too much to sell, there is too much for a buyer—for the advertiser paying for this space—to see. In some sense, digital advertising exists more in theory—that is, it must be somewhere—than in practice.

Sears had to face a salesman's most difficult task: how do you sell what there is too much of?

That is as good a way as any to think about "programmatic" ad sales, the sales methodology that is largely resistant to explanation because it encompasses so many strategies, methods, and intentions, and seems pretty much willing to promise to be anything anyone wants it to be—and that seems certain to be the future basis of all digital media ad sales and to erode ad prices wherever it's implemented.

That last point is also part of the misunderstanding. While

programmatic has certainly lowered the value of digital advertising, programmatic sellers argue that publishers should hire them to bundle their audiences because this will raise their prices.

In a programmatic world, you sell your audience—your clicks, your views, your uniques (or a part thereof)—at a wholesale price to, in effect, a trading desk, with a buy side and a sell side (this is a new unit—a "desk"—at every major advertising and media buying group). The sell side, having bought your traffic, then hands it across the desk to the buy side, which runs a variety of automated trading programs that can deliver preset demographics at preset prices to a client's ad (both buyer and seller can put in a preset bid and ask).

The innovation here is that, as in a stock exchange, there is a constant auction for an audience—that is, really, for a bundled audience, a set of demographic slices aggregated from Web sites far and wide. These audiences are, in a sense, like mortgages, which in the early years of automated finance first started to get bundled together (and then were sold to a consortium of buyers). The other point is that programmatic sellers advanced the notion that you didn't need a particular site or content type or publisher or media entity to reach an audience. It's not the media brand, but an audience's demographic profile, that you are buying.

Digital sellers have long argued the breakthrough efficiency of this way of reaching an audience, but in fact it is an old media form. In the great days of billboards, when American cities and highways were a lush commercial landscape, outdoor advertising, among the cheapest per-eyeball deals you could ever hope to find, were largely sold in packages—you'd get $x$ number of passersby on $x$ number of more or less random billboards for a preset price (the billboard locations defined your demographics).

Anyway, a demographic, as opposed to a self-selected audience (that is, someone specifically choosing to visit your Web site), increases the supply of eyeballs and hence lowers their price. There is a finite amount of *New York Times* readers (although, of course, in the digital world, not that finite) but a much greater number of *New York Times*–type readers (a world of *New York Times*–type readers who rarely read *The New York Times*). Obviously if *New York Times*–type readers are trading at a meaningful discount to actual *New York Times* readers, that might reasonably affect the price of the real thing. And, because many *New York Times* readers, most coming to the *Times* through search engines and other referrals, are not *New York Times* readers in the old sense anyway, their value might reasonably be iffier than it once was.

In the beginning this kind of free-floating inventory was supposed to just be a minor part of what a site might sell. In publishing terms this was remnant space, the leftover stuff. But the amount of digital leftover expanded because the amount of inventory increased and, what's more, premium prices—given the advances of programmatic in the market—and remnant prices began to converge. But never fear, because programmatic sellers were then saying that, with new innovations and enhanced technology, they could now use new targeting methods to raise prices that had fallen. And anyway, while the prices were low, programmatic could give you a guaranteed floor (albeit, of course, a low one), which was better than no floor.

But let's be clear about the essence of the innovation: unbundling the audiences from the brands that had assembled these audiences, and repackaging them as stand-alone unbranded entities, commodified the product, and hence inevitably lowered its price. There were suddenly many entities trying to sell the same commodity, which, with ever-growing digital supply, would force the prices down even more, and, possibly, ever more.

Part of the digital rationale for programmatic is not only that it does provide a greater efficiency but that it would, precisely because it was efficient, come to television too. This was a different argument from the digital position that said digital's price would go up because it could target more efficiently than nondigital media; rather, now the argument was that digital innovations would similarly force the price of all other media down.

There have been, in several heady years of programmatic growth, confident predictions of how much of the ad market would become programmatic—in the telling, practically speaking, all of it.

This was true and yet not true. The true part defined—including in this definition virtually all of digital—a hopelessly glutted and overexpanded advertising market of largely undifferentiated inventory. Buying space in this market was not art, it was process. Programmatic was a better process, one that offered a greater level of consistent control of marketing message as well as measurement of results across all media platforms, and, too, it was one that ought to work as well for undifferentiated television supply. In fact, vast parts of the television day have large amounts of cheap inventory on no-name shows that reach a random audience, in which, as with digital, it's a buyer's market, any price better than no price (after all, once the spot airs, it is forever gone).

But there was another television market that didn't function like this at all. In fact, television has always been a cleanly and cleverly cleaved market, between the junk and the precious, between a glut of commodity space and scarce premium, with the latter providing most of television's profits. In essence, that's what prime time defines.

Even in the most aggressive discussions of programmatic, sought-after television, prime-time television, hit television, a-seller's-market television, and hence most of the value in television, was artfully excluded from the coming promise of programmatic efficiency.

"Nobody can buy, for example, any over-the-air broadcast inventory in these marketplaces [the programmatic marketplaces]— or, of course, anything that is sold during the up-front where ad inventory on new shows is sold at a discount in order to hedge against potential failure, then sold at a large markup in 'scatter' after the season's hits have been established," said Sears in an interview, in an acknowledgment of television's particular economics and the nature of its exclusive product. "It's just not a system that's compatible with the rapid-response ad exchange—and it's how networks amortize the massive costs of programming. It's pricey to option promising properties, produce pilots from a few of them, send a choice few to series, and then give everyone a raise when one or two shows prove to be hits and take a write-off when others tank."

In some sense, the advances of programmatic buying have served to separate the new and efficient—with all its message control and accountability—from the old hat and clumsy, television's old-boy system of backroom deals.

And yet what it also does, in some larger and ironic way, is to further define the dual advertising markets: the downscale market, of commoditized digital audience and junk television, and an upscale, luxury, exclusive television market. The former is bought largely as a pricing function—and with downward price pressure in an ever-expanding market. The latter is a product of limited supply with ever-rising prices.

And that, to a great extent, helps answer that inexplicable and frustrating question for digital people as to why television advertising hasn't followed the American audience to its digital destinations—digital has defined itself as lower-end junk.

# 10

# THE ADVERTISING CURVE

The ultimate end of the media world (or, broader, the modern commercial world) as we know it probably began more recently than with the advent of the Internet. It likely began with the introduction of the DVR in 1999. Both TiVo and ReplayTV (with Marc Andreessen as an investor) launched at the Consumer Electronics Show in Las Vegas in 1999. The premise was to give a viewer control of the TV programming schedule, quite groundbreaking in and of itself, but even more earth-shattering, to provide the technological wherewithal to bypass advertising. Voilà. The media paradigm had been disrupted.

There commenced a long rearguard action to delay the inevitable, but soon enough it was hard not to come to terms with an ultimate nightmare scenario of a world that would no longer willingly tolerate advertising.

Even now, with television's continuing hold on high-priced

advertising, everybody is well aware that it is possible to watch as much television as you'd like without seeing any advertising at all.

Likewise, more and more when you do come upon television advertising, instead of its being a seamless part and parcel of the television experience, a minor toll, it can appear as a quite unnatural and discordant, even fairly incomprehensible, moment—a broken synapse. In other words, there is a growing advertising-free world from which it might not be possible to return to an advertising-ubiquitous world, even for brief visits.

This is partly technology and pricing. Technology enables the unbundling of content from ads (first, rebelliously, through the TV ad-skipping devices, and then officially in OTT—over-the-top content—venues) and new payment options, enabling the consumer to directly pay for content. But it also would be ignoring the obvious not to note that the effectiveness of advertising, that is, traditional, high-margin, display advertising—that builder of brands and creator of desire—has reached some sort of plateau or even a level of net negative impact among jaded media consumers. Every major advertising holding group, those worldwide collections of agencies, marketing services companies, and media buying intermediaries (all with their programmatic buying desks), sees almost all of its growth coming from parts of the world that have only recently become consumer societies. No surprise that advertising tends to work in those markets in the manner it worked here at the dawn of consumer time—it's a cost-effective way to enhance the desire to buy.

Digital advertising works less well even beyond its own clumsy presentation because all advertising works less well, and, alas, digital allows a finer measurement of this ever-falling response rate.

No one in responsible positions in digital or conventional media would, as a function of both fiduciary responsibilities and lack of imagination, openly speculate on the end of their core business basis. And yet it is possible to see most of their efforts at redefinition and future market positioning as a response to the great changes and gradual end to the advertising market as we have known it.

From virtually 100 percent ad supported, television now gets half of its revenues from non-ad businesses—subscription, licensing, foreign sales. At the same time, it retains (and can be expected to maintain) a set of special, high-profile, one-time, real-time, can't-avoid-the-ads events (the Super Bowl first among them, but in a sense all sports), in which advertising's value, against the trends, continues to increase. Television, in a profound sense, no longer sells mere audiences, a game now of commodity and measurement, but rather unique product and cultural currency. In quite an extraordinary development it has converted lowbrow television entertainment, supported indirectly by advertising, into something valuable enough to be directly supported by the consumer and then, as an increasingly valuable currency, traded into one of the fastest-growing business sectors, the new world market for media and entertainment (where, in these markets, it is able to benefit once again from high advertising spending).

In contrast to this model, digital media, disappointed in its efforts to attract a meaningful amount of high-margin brand advertising, has doubled down on its direct-selling advertising abilities, aping the low end of the advertising business—direct-response, call-to-action, act-now advertising.

It's the traditional bifurcation of the media business. On the one hand, there is the influential, the prestigious, the culturally significant, a business and medium of value, need, originality, and exclusivity. On the other hand, there's the cheap, crass, and low, a constant and immediate arbitrage between what you spend to create the medium against the short-term sales it produces. One side of the business produces content meant to stand on its own (the content is the asset), another side makes the circulars, direct mail, advertorial, freestanding inserts (the junk in Sunday papers), telemarketing calls, crap magazines, and cable ads that in the end only justify the creation of the ad rather than any independent-value content. It's all media, but with fundamentally different models and to a different effect.

Facebook's value as a technology company may seem high, but its actual value comes from the enormity of its meaningless, undifferentiated traffic. It has no other product it can sell than some ads next to complaints about neighbors' dogs, party pics, and humblebrags.

There are different degrees of acknowledging advertising's dominance over content, from a defiant pretense otherwise (travel magazines, for instance), to the direct mail business, where there is no pretense. But the spectrum forms the essence of the media business—and most everyone, at some level, knows where they fall on it.

Except when they don't.

What would otherwise be hack publishing can, in this new environment, appear to be a great experiment in an evolving market. Unlike any other medium, generating traffic, any kind of traffic, doesn't tarnish prestige; it creates it.

The digital media circumstance, in almost every instance where there is not meaningful subscription revenue (and there are few such instances), is a classic schlock model: advertising priced on the basis of its measurable response and immediate sales performance means low per-user revenues means cheap content—content that effectively converges into advertising (e.g., *BuzzFeed*'s "native content"). The only thing that truly distinguishes it from the cheap direct-response publishing model of long standing is the belief that technology has made such businesses almost infinitely scalable. *BuzzFeed* (or, for that matter, Facebook) may have a low-value user base, but it can grow one of almost infinite size.

There is, in entrepreneurial fashion, quite a bit of fake-it-till-we-make-it hopefulness here. *BuzzFeed*, with its massive traffic growth fueled by its schlock skills, nevertheless touts the journalism it also tries to produce. (It's a kind of kids' version of the early CBS strategy, using its "Tiffany Network" image for news to offset what was arguably the nadir of prime-time programming, including *The Beverly Hillbillies* and *Hogan's Heroes*.) The ultimate hope here is that, at some tipping point, a different kind of advertising, one not based on immediate response but on investing in shifts of mood, opinion, desire, of creating the grand illusions and stories that propel consumer life—and big media margins—will migrate to *BuzzFeed* and to Facebook from television.

But the cycle is not going to be an easy one to break.

Digital media has created, perhaps inexorably, an ever-larger, ever-more-low-value audience. As a response to this, or in tandem with this, advertising agencies have de-emphasized, even hollowed out, what had been their core talent and purpose—crafting vivid and theatrical consumer fantasies—in favor of being operators that profit off the transaction of ad placement, the measurement of response, and even the facilitation of payment.

As the head of a big digital agency said to me: "We don't do story. We facilitate the handshake by moving the cash register closer to the consumer. That's much more economical and efficient than trying to create demand and desire."

In other words, the ultimate result is that there will be no advertising, not advertising of the kind that believed in investing large amounts of money to transform attitudes and behavior. Instead there will be more process and efficiency, the stuff that technology is good at, but that undermines the uniqueness of media and hence its value.

# PART 4

# COUNTER-REVOLUTION

## 11

# THE NETFLIX *UN*REVOLUTION

The solipsism of the tech community sees Netflix as a satisfying disruption of the TV business. But that's a striking inversion of what's actually happening: TV is disrupting the Internet.

It is not Netflix bringing digital to television, but, quite obviously, Netflix bringing television programming and values and behavior—like passive watching—to heretofore interactive and computing-related screens.

Netflix was a commerce company delivering DVDs, no more part of the media business, or show business, than Blockbuster, the video rental company that once had outposts in strip malls everywhere. But this early origin and business model (you paid them) became the crucial difference in its efforts to break out of the fulfillment business—the need to get paid (or the habit of being paid) pushed Netflix beyond the limitations of digital media.

This was mostly a happenstance segue. Netflix initially was

not going into the media business. Rather, it was a disrupter of retail models, first delivering DVDs by mail, offering a larger selection and lower cost, and then delivering the same product via new streaming technology. Both advances transformed the video rental market. But the perception in the marketplace and at Netflix that this further advance had moved it from the retail business and into the realm of HBO and premium paid television was after the fact, a dawning realization.

Mirabile dictu: Netflix was the first successful seller of content in the digital world. It proved the subscription model.

And one more unwitting breakthrough: Up until Netflix, television had always been organized on a geographical model. Networks were an association of local affiliates; cable systems, even consolidated ones, were a collection of exclusive licenses to wire specific communities; cable stations lived or died on their ability to make deals with local cable franchises. And, of course, none of this transcended national borders.

Netflix, on the other hand, implemented its streaming service—pivotally with a third-party license of content through Starz, a second-level cable pay-TV service—on a national basis overnight.

Internet protocol (IP) destroyed the myth of television localism—and that there were daunting hurdles in creating a television network.

There was one more crucial aspect to Netflix's transformation into media, and its lightning rise to a competitive television network: its CEO, Reed Hastings.

Hastings is . . . a salesman. He describes himself in all the ways that tech guys like to describe themselves, as an entrepreneur, as an engineer, as someone surely with the temperament of a technical and software visionary. But really what distinguishes Hastings is that he sells. He courts; he schmoozes; he begs. He has built what he would like to characterize as a tech company not as tech companies are built, on platform functionality, but as media companies are built, on his ability to make deals and then trade up to better deals.

Curiously, among the many formative moments in the company's development, the loss of its Starz deal, which gave it a trove of movie licenses, a seemingly certain setback, encouraged it to make a different kind of deal that would transform it once again: Netflix had to license television programs. And rather within a blink of an eye, it went from being a feature film rental site (a few million people a day go to the movies) to being a rerun television network (40 to 50 million people a night watch television).

It not only became a de facto television channel, it established the crossover market of licensing deals for television shows. Television's major, if not singular, preoccupation—looking for downstream markets for its product—suddenly had another outlet. Not only was digital, in this regard, not competitive with television, it was a wholly unexpected expansion of ancillary revenue. Digital became part of the television business. An additional Netflix contribution was to turn heretofore ad-support network shows into paid products too.

Reed Hastings and Netflix, surprising nobody so much as themselves, woke up as a television channel. Other than being delivered via IP, Netflix had almost nothing to do with the conventions of digital media—in a sense it rejected them. It is not user generated, it is not social, it is not bite size, it is not free. It is in every way, except for its route into people's homes—and the differences here would soon get blurry—the same as television. It was old-fashioned, passive, narrative entertainment.

When it began its move into original programming it rushed to say, in an effort to project its technology bona fides, that its user data gave it the wherewithal to more finely calibrate the market, the zeitgeist, and the chances for a hit. Many press accounts of *House of Cards*, its first original production, had it as the miraculous result of a big data, big brother confection of heretofore unimagined audience research. In fact, it was a project that its producer and star, Kevin Spacey, had been shopping to all the major television outlets. It landed at Netflix because it had been unsuccessful in finding another home. Its success was an example not of data, but in classic television and show business fashion, the caprice and luck of a needy buyer meeting an eager seller.

Netflix had merely recreated the premium channel television business, in its economic and narrative structure, different only in the way that it had established a third distribution track. There was broadcast, cable, and, after Netflix, IP (or OTT), but surely this was more an expanding television business rather than an expanding digital business. There was, in fact, rather little that Netflix depended on from the digital system of networked traffic and advertising revenue, whereas it was entirely dependent on its ability to license television content and to attract top writing, acting, producing, and directing talent.

And yet Netflix became a new digital standard-bearer. In 2014 a *New Yorker* profile effectively made Netflix the official television killer (there have been many prior television killers). Auletta, writing about the media business for many decades, is surely the voice of the establishment in the field, conferring dominance to the players he covers. Very little in this particular piece was new. Rather, the approach here—putting a lot of well-known sources on the record in support of the current and popular thesis—is meant to solidify, rather than challenge, a widespread impression, and to thereby stand as the definitive statement. It is an instructive example of a kind of Silicon Valley agitprop that is so often retailed through traditional reporters and that then becomes the conventional wisdom adopted by the financial community as well as by other journalists.

"Television," says Auletta, as his pro forma thesis, "is undergoing a digital revolution."

"We are to cable networks as cable networks were to broadcast networks," Auletta quotes Hastings. And yet cable, far from overthrowing television, vastly expanded the television business. "It's like little termites eating away," Auletta quotes Jason Hirschhorn, a cable executive who has tried to migrate into the digital business, and who is best known as one of the last executives to run doomed Myspace. "I don't think," says Hirschhorn, who has not worked in either the digital or cable industry since his Myspace debacle, "the incumbents are insecure enough."

Auletta recapitulates television history as the story of the center not holding ever since the three broadcast networks were challenged by cable (Auletta wrote a book in the 1980s about this scary moment for the networks), when in fact the story, far from old broadcast losing to new cable, was the creation of a vast new system of added revenues and cross-ownership.

*First came cable-television networks, which delivered HBO, ESPN, CNN, Nickelodeon, and dozens of other channels through a coaxial*

*cable. Cable operators and networks charged monthly fees and sold ads,*
*and even commercial-free premium networks such as HBO made money*
*for cable operators, because they attracted subscribers. Traditional*
*broadcasters saw their advertising income slow, but they compensated by*
*charging cable companies for carrying their content, a "retransmission*
*consent" fee made possible, in 1992, by the Cable Television Consumer*
*Protection and Competition Act. Soon after, the F.C.C. relaxed rules*
*that restricted the networks' ownership of prime-time programs, which*
*opened a new stream of revenue from the syndication of their shows to*
*local stations, cable networks, and other platforms.*

This is, in tone, peculiarly cast as a negative, as a descent, or at
best a holding-on by the fingernails, instead of the virtual definition of a growth business, and even a reborn industry.

"The advent of the Internet and streaming video brought new
competitors," Auletta continues, skipping over about twenty years
of television growth.

He then offers a paean to YouTube: "YouTube makes money
through what Robert Kyncl, a vice-president at Google and the
head of content and business operations at YouTube, calls 'friction-
less' advertising, which allows viewers to click on a TrueView but-
ton to skip ads and asks advertisers to pay only when viewers watch
the ad." In fact, YouTube, to the continuing distress of Google, has
consistently failed to break into television's advertising market.

*"We now live in a world where every device is a television," Richard Green-*
*field, a media and technology analyst for the New York–based B.T.I.G.,*
*told me. "TV is just becoming video. My kids watch 'Good Luck Charlie' on*
*Netflix. To my ten-year-old, that's TV." Consumers don't care "that a show*

*is scheduled at eight o'clock," he said. Paul Saffo, a Silicon Valley technol-*
*ogy forecaster, says that couch potatoes have given way to "active hunters,"*
*viewers who "snack" and control what they watch and when.*

Beyond the fact that the experts here are two of the most promiscuous quoters, invariably on point for a given thesis, what is to be made of the notion that *TV is just becoming video*? Quite as truly video is TV and, clearly, digital media is becoming video, therefore digital media is TV.

Auletta then gives a poor-rich-boy treatment to CBS chairman Les Moonves, the most well-compensated executive in television. The implication is that Rome burns while Moonves is paid, and yet, as though in deadpan support of his own larger point about video undergoing a digital revolution, Auletta adds that CBS's share price was twenty times higher than at its lowest point in 2009 and that almost half of its revenues come "from its overseas sales, which totaled $1.1 billion last year, and from licensing deals with cable and digital platforms such as Verizon FiOS and Netflix; Netflix pays CBS and Fox about two hundred and fifty million dollars each to let it air programs from their archives."

This last is something of a diss at CBS's falling advertising market, which in fact has remained relatively stable while adding a powerful nonadvertising income stream.

Then Marc Andreessen, in his role as prominent digital proselytizer (and with his slate of investments dependent on this view of digital's leveling of the old world), is up in Auletta's narrative:

*The venture capitalist Marc Andreessen, who co-invented Mosaic, the*
*first commercial Internet browser—it later became Netscape—told me,*

*"TV in ten years is going to be one hundred per cent streamed. On de-*
*mand. Internet Protocol. Based on computers and based on software."*
*He said that the television industry has managed the transition to the*
*digital age better than book publishers and music executives, but "soft-*
*ware is going to eat television in the exact same way, ultimately, that*
*software ate music and as it ate books."*

Even to the degree this absolute vision is true (no more broadcast, no more cable, through which, of course, streaming is possible), software is neither going to create television comedies and
dramas nor change the underlying licensing or advertising structure of the business.

And then finally Auletta gets to Netflix as exhibit A in television's video revolution. And yet his revolution is immediately reduced to Netflix's efforts not to change the nature of the business,
but in fact to find its place in it:

*Hastings sees his main competitors as Showtime and, especially, HBO.*
*Both have lucrative arrangements with cable providers, through which*
*they offer a library of shows and movies to watch on demand; and both*
*now offer apps—HBO Go and Showtime Anytime—that enable cable*
*subscribers to watch any of those channels' programs on any device.*
*HBO has more than two and a half times as many subscribers world-*
*wide as Netflix—a hundred and fourteen million—and its list of origi-*
*nal hits, from "The Sopranos" to "Game of Thrones," is extensive.*

Then Auletta winds up for his knockout punch: the television
advertising model is teetering, he says, because people now have

the technology to skip ads. Martin Sorrell, chairman of WPP, the world's largest advertising agency holding company (Auletta says it's the second largest), tells Auletta that WPP has moved a big chunk of its spending to digital. And then, says Auletta, Netflix and other streaming services offer an existential challenge to television. Why watch the box and subscribe to cable when there are so many other options?

First, almost the entirety of digital media is advertising supported (ads that are far easier to skip and to ignore than those on television), save only for Netflix and other streaming services that charge for television content. Second, television, once wholly advertising driven, now derives 50 percent of its revenue from other sources—not that it has lost 50 percent of its advertising revenue, but rather that it has effectively doubled its revenue from non-ad sources. (NYU Stern School professor Scott Galloway argues that the healthiest media companies will have a revenue base that is evenly split between advertising and other licensing and subscription revenue streams.) What's more, the Martin Sorrell point means virtually the opposite of what Auletta suggests: the overwhelming amount of advertising dollars that have moved into digital have not come from television budgets; in addition, this money has been parceled out in low-value increments that have hobbled rather than fueled the digital revolution.

As for the existential specter of Netflix, what Auletta and *The New Yorker* describe sounds a lot like an ever-expanding market for television's product, and not, per se, much like competition. As for cable, again, how is it that streaming happens?

The challenge for television is not the Netflix model; rather, the challenge for Netflix is to figure out how to adopt more of a television model. On similar earnings, HBO's net operating profit in 2013 was $1.8 billion, while Netflix's was a mere $0.62 billion. This is largely because, in its over-the-top assault, it doesn't have cable companies picking up much of the cost of marketing, billing, and service.

What Netflix needs is a cable deal.

# 12

# SCREEN TIME

It isn't really computing that rescues Apple from its 1990s decline when Steve Jobs returns to run the company; it's entertainment. First it's music. Apples saves the music business from chaos, and then puts it into a kind of receivership, making it dependent on its device, the iPod, and its store, iTunes. And then, in one of the most far-ranging revolutions in the media industry perhaps since the advent of television itself, it makes portable screens ubiquitous.

In this, Apple has had two goals. The first was an extraordinary success: piggyback off ever-growing media demand and create devices that become a necessary part of that market. The second has been less successful: achieve some point of significant control in this market—to do for video what it did in music.

Jobs ought rightly to be regarded as much as a media figure as a computing giant. Jay Chiat, whose advertising agency Chiat/Day created the Apple Big Brother 1984 spot, and was Jobs's longtime friend and confidant, described—in many discussions we had about Apple before Chiat's death in 2002—Jobs's relative lack of interest in technology figures and obsessive and competitive interest in movie and television moguls. Most of Jobs's personal fortune, amassed after his return to Apple, came from his investment in the animation studio Pixar, and its eventual sale to Disney. His early motivations and sensibility are more pop culture than data driven. He's impresario-like. He's top-down. He's message, not process. He's a control freak. What set Jobs apart from the competition was his ability to create a narrative—often with Chiat's help—about his products when the competitors were churning out soulless gray boxes.

Instead of his mobile machines becoming new venues of extended functionality—walking computers, taking the desktop with you—they became a new proscenium, a new way to frame pastimes and entertainment, designed for distraction as much as for usefulness (perhaps more for distraction).

Jobs himself was, relatively speaking, anti-Web. He was rather the last guy who would be at home in an unruly, contributory environment. He was basically an old-fashioned, ever-controlling, hopelessly obsessive media mogul. It was his way. It's a closed system. Or, in a better metaphor, it's his theater and his show. (He really was a mogul.)

Apple may be the most valuable company in America, but it did not get there by selling ads. It makes things and sells things, which is very different from everyone else in the *BuzzFeed* bubble, including Facebook and Google (though even Google seems to realize this, putting more effort into Android than new Web products).

The introduction of the iPhone and then iPad is an important moment in which the cultural onrush of the Web, of its seeming octopus grasp of all experience, information, and functionality, is slowed and challenged: Apple mobile devices establish their own parallel world. Apps compete with, and to some extent sideline, the Web.

His is, Jobs explicitly argues, a better media world—and a better world *for* media. His self-serving pitch to the media industry is that he can give back control over look and feel; he can control access; he can police the environment; he can design the experience; he can dictate the business model. At this point, beginning with the iPhone in 2007 and extending to the iPad in 2010, the media business is in full panic over the digital maelstrom. Jobs was saying the deluge could be controlled and that he was the man to do it. He was the alternative.

Eddy Cue, a twenty-year Apple veteran, with no presence in the media industry and, indeed, hardly any presence anywhere— he's even a social media blank—became Apple's intractable and fearsome negotiator, though of the more take-it-or-leave-it than getting-to-yes type. ("An inflexible and unpredictable negotiator who frequently reverses and contradicts himself," according to *Adweek* magazine, which described a negotiation for media content in which Cue suddenly decided content creators ought to "use Apple's own terms-of-service agreement, designed for software developers.")

What Jobs had in mind, surely, was, in addition to selling vast quantities of units, an über–distribution control. The music business, helpless in the digital deluge, granted Jobs and Apple something like surrender terms in its arrangement with iTunes.

That example was already frighteningly clear to the larger media business. Rupert Murdoch came back from his first look at the iPad and reported, "This thing could screw everybody if we're not careful."

But Jobs's devices had reduced—finally reduced—the digital world to a straight distribution deal. However hard the negotiation was, it ultimately ran up against the need for brand-name content—that was what made the iPad different from a laptop.

This was not an inverted world where producers gave up control and audiences assumed it. This was not a Google appropriation by a thousand cuts, give them an inch and they'll take a fair-use mile. This was not tools over entertainment (tools that so often became the means to claim and redistribute entertainment). This was wholly familiar licensing and distribution—the two pillars of the media business. (Although magazines rushed into this new channel, they were hobbled both by an advertiser lack of interest and by the need for constant technological improvement; video, on the other hand, was neither dependent on advertising nor on upgrades.)

In the first, a third party paid you for the use of your intellectual property in ways that were, quite unlike the unruly Web, precisely defined, representing a half century of media art and custom. In the second, you paid a third party to help bring you to a preestablished audience: movies need movie theater chains; television producers needed broadcast networks and then cable operators. Again, these were the defining relationships and deal structures of the business. Where they were hellishly disrupted by the Web, these business relationships were largely restored by Apple's screens.

Apple had become a licensing organization. And, too, it had become a distributor of apps that had struck their own licensing agreements. Jobs's screens became a predictable and legitimized world of content distribution.

Still, the nature of the device, and how behavior would adapt to it, remained uncertain. In the consumer mind would these be primarily computing devices or entertainment devices—for various information processing tasks, even for general communication and social media interactions, or passive content transmission tools? How would the pie divide?

What market did they expand?

The tablet's initial strategy, and raison d'être, was as an incursion into the living room, a kind of personal television and games console, ideally an Apple-controlled personal television and games console, an effort on Apple's part to pull the center of gravity away from the television itself and from television distribution (a better gamble than its continuing efforts at a set-top box). But, in fact, in some sense use shifted in the other way: tablets, especially in the younger market, started to replace PCs. It even seemed to appear that instead of becoming an entertainment device, tablets would merely become a lower-cost computing device.

But, more unexpected, both things happened: tablets and smart phones (with constantly expanding screen sizes) became entertainment devices that end up taking over PC functionality. In other words, they become incursions into the office and computing. With a little critical interpretation, television comes to the computer, and not, as had long been predicted, the other way around (that previous notion was WebTV—you'd browse the Web and do e-mail and perform other computing functions on a big screen from your couch).

It's an elemental point: the television does not become a

computing device; the various computing devices become remarkably satisfactory entertainment devices, not just making entertainment available at any time and in any place but pushing entertainment—professionally made, scripted narratives—into the realm of digital activity.

The devices themselves mean that digital media executives become as reliant—or more reliant—on writers, actors, directors, and producers as on programmers.

# 13

# MORE BOXES

"Digital convergence" turns out not so much to be about bringing computing to your television but about bringing more television to your television.

Accept that the medium is the message (in Douglas Coupland's succinct explanation of Marshall McLuhan's still opaque aphorism—more than half a century later still opaque: "The ostensible content of all electronic media is insignificant; it is the medium *itself* that has the greater impact on the environment, a fact bolstered by the now medically undeniable fact that the technologies we use every day begin, after a while, to alter the way our brains work, and hence the way we experience the world"), but what is the medium?

The box, that retro term of objectification and dismissal of television, that dominating presence in living rooms for half a century, has new, more fluid meaning, in the myriad, mostly boxlike devices that move digital video from the Internet to the television.

We are in a land of curious metaphors. There is the suggestion that television is one world and the digital realm another—and in the minds of most users that is probably true. In that view, there are two routes for video into the home, the first by some conventional, limited, old-fashioned, literal, and hardwired cable, and the second, more mysteriously, "over the top (OTT)," coming from the cloud or other cyber provinces. (In the past, there was broadcast, which came, in a sense more magically, over the air—but broadcast of course now comes over cable, as does, in fact, OTT.)

And then there is a conjunction in the middle—with a box or boxes. One box gives you cable. Another box moves video from the cyber world onto the television. True, some boxes do both things, or at least provide an intersection for both functions. But, notionally, there are separate streams converging through discrete boxes to the central box.

At the same time, there is a reverse process that is also over the top, which, in another set of complicated procedures and behind-the-scenes maneuvers, moves video, heretofore exclusive to the television, out into the cloudy cyber world. Hence, now retrievable on your computer and other devices and secondary screens, but, confusingly, also reroutable by your streaming box back to your television.

Functionally, this just defines the ubiquitous availability of video content, except that, changing the nature of the game, it also sets up exclusive channels of content, such that we now lack an overall metaphor for the experience. It is no longer television that gives us, well, television. It is no longer cable that gives us a cable system with its basic and premium options. It is something else that gives us access to this division of television, or to this addition to television, or to this particular television licensing organization, but not to another competing television licensing organization.

Behind vast new programming options, through this multi-tiered system of licensing and technology, there are of course new power centers and new points of leverage in the system, as well as new innovations in watching, retrieving, saving, and finding. In addition to there being many OTT options and approaches competing against one another, they are all, in theory, competing against television system monopolies (i.e., cable companies), except that because there aren't, in actuality, two routes into your home, but only one broadband line, transporting both television video and digital video, they are all entirely dependent on the broadband owner, who also maintains the television monopoly.

But still the basic questions apply: Does this really change television, or is it just more of the same (although this just-more-of-the-same was always the charge against cable, and cable in fact did change television)? Does it give someone else real power in the game? Does it favor distributor or maker? Does it further fracture or further consolidate the industry, or both? And does the consumer ever really catch a break?

The short primer:

"Streaming media devices"—as they are increasingly referred to—include far more varied options than just stand-alone units like an Apple TV or a Roku. There are more than fifty such devices applying various approaches currently on the market. But whatever we call them and however they're configured, the key component of each device is that: 1) it's IP-capable (whether via an Ethernet port or Wi-Fi); 2) it connects to your TV; 3) it can install apps for a variety of streaming services that you can navigate via an interface similar to, but fortunately simpler than, a PC operating system.

One bit of research in 2014 estimated the market penetration of the stand-alone devices in U.S. homes at 17 percent. (Apple TV and Roku are at the moment the current market leaders by far, with Apple's device holding a 39 percent market share, and Roku 28 percent.) This study forecasts a 39 percent market penetration by 2017 for all devices in the category. In other words, adaptation is happening here faster than cable penetrated U.S. households.

Google and Amazon are both making major moves into this market. Google is doing it via its Chromecast device as well as its new Android TV platform (an adaptation of the Android operating system that is being used by third-party manufacturers, similar to the way smart phone makers use Android for mobile but, of course, designed to be viewed from across the room rather than up close). Chromecast is one of several new stick or dongle streaming media devices that plug directly into an HDMI port on your television, rather than being connected to a separate box via a cable. Amazon, meanwhile, now has the Amazon Fire TV, which uses an Amazon-developed OS adapted from Android.

Beyond these stand-alone devices, a number of other home A/V-type components are also now capable of delivering streaming media. TiVo, one of the earlier leaders in the DVR market, has added the ability to deliver streaming apps to its most recent devices. The same is true for Sony's PlayStation, Nintendo's Wii, and Microsoft's Xbox platforms (with Sony recently adding a stripped-down PlayStation TV device to its product line).

But a far larger potential user base includes IP-capable Blu-ray

DVD players, which have been in the market for several years now (an estimated 169 million in the U.S. market as of 2014), as well as the so-called smart TVs, which are rapidly entering it.

Then, too, it is probably an unnecessary limitation to consider this market just devices that can connect to your TV (or may in fact *be* your TV). In many ways, the media streaming universe—the over-the-top content world—includes anything with an IP connection that can play video: tablet, smart phone, set-top box, dongle, computer, and television. One analyst put the total shipment of all OTT-capable devices in 2013 at 1.67 billion.

We are not in Kansas anymore.

Or are we?

The early assumption about IP-connected television devices was that it would bring the Web to your TV, a kind of futuristic, interactive big brother on your wall. As in the original Internet construct, it was about opening a further larger window into a new, surround-sound, 3D, information world— *Matrix*-like stuff. We would run our lives and interact with the world through a TV-like monitor. (In fact, this rather turned out to be the realm, in smaller form, of the phone.) Almost nobody imagined that the television would become yet a greater platform and showcase for conventional, beginning-middle-end entertainment. And yet, in a development that ought to be confusing to every futurist, television, occupying more, not less, individual daily attention, has remained almost wholly an entertainment device. What's more, other than games, which have become ever more video-like and video-inspired, the form of television entertainment has stayed remarkably the same: three scripted acts, with designated players. Even unscripted "reality" television, that money-saving response to fracturing audiences, has become increasingly structured and, in fact, scripted.

OTT devices, instead of becoming a way to bring the new interactive digital world to television, became a way to bring more television to television. And, too, they have become a back door into the television business. Amazon, Apple, and Google—distributors and potential programmers (Amazon is already a serious programmer)—are in the OTT business not just to facilitate their streaming products and services, but as a way to stake a claim on television territory too, each with network-like ambitions, or fantasies.

Aereo, an audacious and harebrained start-up, proposed to use an OTT device to, in effect, restore original broadcast television. Its scheme was to rent you a remote antenna that would in old-fashioned form deliver you broadcast television stations, allowing you to bypass cable fees—or, that is, to pay Aereo a lower fee for the broadcast signals it was sucking from air and delivering back to your television over the Internet. This was a notion, cheered by the digital side, that traveled quickly to the Supreme Court, where it was made mincemeat by television's collective legal mind and might.

Aereo's fallback position was to join a range of other such start-ups and use the OTT route to the television as an orderly and legal licensing method to simply deliver television programming as it now exists—but with the added value of a better interface and searching tools. That is, television is not changed, nor its value diminished, but rather the promise is to enhance it. (In fact, finding this market already crowded, Aereo accepted defeat and folded.)

This is, of course, at a cost. "Pure" OTT bundles that would essentially replace what a viewer gets from his or her cable or satellite provider may well end up costing more than the original package—in a continuing effort to test the upper range (so far unreached) of the consumer's willingness to pay for television. What's more, these new bundles, while seeming to threaten cable, may be a boon to it. Charter Communications CEO Tom Rutledge seemed barely able to contain himself at a 2013 analyst conference, pointing out that the Internet access business (and no matter what OTT device you might have, you will need Internet access, most likely through a cable provider) has higher margins than the traditional cable television business, and that an ever more fractured field of content providers increased cable's leverage with the individual players. (Of course, the content providers, given new ways into the home, argue the same thing about cable.)

Smart TVs, trying to incorporate new capabilities, continue to threaten the individual solutions. But at least in the near term, as much as some people might want to get rid of the box or multiple boxes under their TVs, many also prefer the ability to swap devices in and out when there are improvements in the technology. Cheaper to replace a box than the whole television. Also, the stand-alone boxes usually have more custom capabilities—the ability to act as media hubs if you have multiple TVs in the house, for instance—as well as better interfaces for surfing or searching through programming. For someone who has accumulated a large library of videos and music via iTunes, for example, Apple TV is going to give you a far greater ability to view that stuff on your TV, or listen via your stereo. Roku, on the other hand, prides itself on its cross-platform search tools, allowing you to better hunt for a particular show you want to watch on any of the streaming services you subscribe to.

Another range-war aspect of the OTT future is an effort, in effect, to repeat the early television model and create exclusive programming in order to sell hardware and technology. In this high-stakes world, specific boxes or connections will provide specific entertainment packages. As HBO was a premium channel, now, potentially, there is a world of premium boxes, which may both give you what you cannot get from other competitive services and cut you off from what you might want from other services as well—all, naturally, heating up the competitive landscape for programmers and program makers, as well as distributors, and naturally presaging a certain wave of consolidation.

Still, the medium likely needs a new and improved metaphor—consolivision?

# 14

# CONSOLIDATING CONSOLIVISION

It was a curiously winding road for the television business to actually understand it was in the television business.

Starting in the 1980s, the idea of the "media business" became something like a unified field theory. Except, in fact, there was little unified about this business. There were publishing businesses and there were entertainment businesses. There were movies, supported by ticket sales; there was television, supported by advertising. There were large consumer magazines supported by national advertising; there were newspapers supported by local retailers and classified listings. There was a production business, and then a mostly separate distribution arm. There were books, a unit sale business. There was radio. There were billboards. Even a classical theory of horizontal integration wasn't going to bring many of these disparate disciplines into alignment or a logical relationship.

It wasn't so much a theory or a plan as it was the ability to finance acquisitions that brought the whole lot together. It was a grand scheme of opportunity and dominance, most of all envisioned by Rupert Murdoch, who, in addition to having the appetite and imagination, had, with his base in Australia, and his ambitions around the world, an accounting trick to finance it all. Under Australian accounting rules, aspects of what would otherwise be regarded as debt were regarded as equity—hence you could continue to borrow against it—and the value of "goodwill" remained on your balance sheet and was not, as it is under standard rules, depreciated.

In little more than a decade, he transformed his company from a newspaper publisher to an international magazine, television, movie, satellite, and book company, creating, from a hodgepodge of largely unrelated businesses, the media business.

A series of competitors followed suit, gathering virtually all movie studios; television networks and stations; major book, magazine, and newspaper publishers; cable programmers and cable and satellite systems; and, too, radio networks and billboards companies, comprising hundreds if not thousands of separate entities, under the effective control of a handful of companies: Time Warner, Disney, Viacom, News Corp, Comcast (magazines and newspapers were consolidated under Advance–Condé Nast, Hearst, Tribune, Gannett, and radio under Clear Channel).

There were a variety of screwball rationales to this. There was the one broadly known as synergy—companies that both performed different functions or that were competitive with each other would work together—that would quickly become a punch line. And then there was the visualization that saw audiences fracturing but being regathered by merely buying them back as they spread—an improbable notion, which, anyway, soon met the Web.

Digital competition, changes in the advertising market, the collapse of the music and print industries, and the fracturing of television had, over the last ten years, both a paralyzing and transformative effect on these big companies. They were paralyzed because vast parts of their empires were under siege—clear to all, these outposts would be lost. Beyond managing decline, and hoping for some fortuitous intersection with digital media (Time Warner lost five years in its merger with AOL; Viacom fired its CEO, Tom Freston, for not buying Myspace, while News Corp bought Myspace, only to see it, in a matter of months, lose its dominance to Facebook and go out of business), nobody could really have described a plausible growth model and glowing future.

They transformed by the almost random dumb luck of television's dual revenue stream.

This happens almost in an unconscious or happenstance fashion. Disney becomes the dominant media company because, in its 1995 acquisition of ABC, it also got ESPN, an insignificant add-on that would become the most valuable cable station. Hearst, which owns 20 percent of ESPN, and, in addition, 50 percent of A&E (Disney owning the other 50 percent), was lifted from the fading fortunes of magazines and the dismal fate of its newspapers. Time Warner dumped its music business (Warner Music), its Internet business (AOL), its book business (Warner Books and Little, Brown), its cable system (Time Warner Cable), and its magazine company (Time Inc.), keeping only HBO, Turner Broadcasting, and the Warner Bros. movie studio—and, in the process, doubling its value. Advance Communications's 31 percent passive interest in the Discovery Channel is now worth more than its newspaper chain (the fourth largest in the United States by circulation) and its

Condé Nast magazine group put together. Viacom split off CBS, its low-growth network business (including in it its book business), from its fast-growing cable channel businesses (including MTV, VH1, Comedy Central, and BET Networks), but then CBS, by grabbing a piece of cable fees for itself, also vaulted forward. Rupert Murdoch, the first media conglomerator, whose newspapers formed the backbone of his company and his personal interest, was forced by the scandals involving his London papers to separate the troubled papers from the thriving entertainment company. Largely against his will, his company was split in 2013 into News Corp, holding the legacy publishing interests in the United States, United Kingdom, and Australia, and 21st Century Fox, with the Fox Network, cable stations (Fox News, FX, Fox Sports Network), movie studio, and its 39 percent controlling interest in Sky TV, the British Satellite Network. Fox's value minus the value of its worldwide newspapers and as a pure-play television company climbed more than 20 percent over the next year.

It is arguably only at this point, with 21st Century Fox a separate company forging its own strategy, that the new old media model becomes clear. If Murdoch invented the unified field theory of media consolidation, in which anything that could plausibly be called media became media, he was now concisely acknowledging the new field theory: media is television. (Murdoch has had a long and hapless history with digital media, including buying the first consumer-access Internet provider, Delphi, the then largest social network, Myspace, and launching the first tablet-only newspaper, *The Daily*. Each of these gambits was, in its own way, a disaster, sending him, chastened, back to his true business.)

Accordingly, Murdoch's 21st Century Fox, now close to a pure-play broadcast and cable television programming company, offers to buy Time Warner, another pure-play television programming company.

Murdoch, quite unique among the figures who have shaped the television business, is not a television guy. He's never made television, never sold it, never been truly part of the industry that does. In fact, he's never really watched television. He's even largely left Fox News to Roger Ailes. Murdoch would really not know the first thing about making a news show, or any show. He's a newspaperman. And partly because newspapering is, for him, a process of judging and manipulating who has power, and, in that process, creating power for himself, he has developed a preternatural instinct for those two central public pillars, politics and media.

Emerging out of the 2008 financial meltdown and the long recession, the strength of cable television became clear not just against the decline of almost all other media, but in and of itself, as a business in an exceptional position: cable customer fees continued to climb and, even amid continual complaints, did not reach even a sense of ceiling—hence, cable licensing and retransmission fees rose too; television advertising became ever stronger—given the Internet alternative, you could even say there was a flight to television.

If Murdoch himself is temperamentally of a pre-television age, his daughter Elisabeth and his son James are consummate television executives and provide, in an almost spooky generational melding, something of an additional consciousness for him. He is, in a sense, able to process their experience as his own. Elisabeth has, after quitting his company in a huff in the late nineties, built one of the largest international production companies, not just making and acquiring shows, but creating and licensing "formats," a new marketplace wherein underlying narrative structures and techniques (e.g., gimmicks) are bought and sold. James ran BSkyB (from 2003 to 2007), the British satellite broadcaster, which more and more has become a key component of the Murdoch growth strategy. The Murdochs own 39 percent of the company. It is in part their efforts to buy the entire company that leads to the backlash in the United Kingdom that helps fuel the hacking scandal, which results in the quashing of the BSkyB deal, the splitting of the company, and the renewed effort to double down on television in the form of Time Warner.

In one sense, the merger's rationale is to build a better, more ultimate bulwark against the looming distributor conglomerate of Comcast and its impending combination with Time Warner Cable. That is, the more good video assets you own, the more necessary you are to do business with, the more leverage that gives you, the more your relationship becomes negotiable rather than take it or leave it.

But it is also a pure, giddy sense of opportunity, the thing that most moves Murdoch. In part because of the Comcast consolidation, but in part because of the expanding television business—that is, a vast, growing consumer appetite—Murdoch foresees a new age of media (that is, television) consolidation, raising asset value across the television spectrum.

And if he controls a lion's share of the sweetest assets, and Time Warner would have made 21st Century Fox the dominant cable programming company (what's more, Fox's sports assets with Time Warner's sports assets would make a formidable ESPN competitor), then his assets would rise the most in value.

How can he not play?

But in fact, it turns out he may be too late. His bid for Time

Warner may have confirmed television's pure-play strength, but the market may be close behind if not even with him.

His own shareholders, driving down 21st Century Fox's share price after the bid, clearly feel the assets are powerful enough that, to get them, Murdoch is going to have to pay a substantial premium. What's more, Time Warner shareholders, even looking at a premium bid from Murdoch, seem perfectly willing to believe TW CEO Jeffrey Bewkes that, in the relative short term, he can raise the value to well beyond Murdoch's already rich offer.

Effectively priced out of the market, Murdoch withdraws his offer. It's a bitter blow. His timing is usually more prescient than this. But now everybody seems to know television's value. What's more, everybody knows that Murdoch's restless appetites and long history of never leaving the fight mean his own interest will help keep values high.

Rather miraculously, the entire idea of media (that is, television) conglomerates seems back in vogue, along with media moguls, energized by—along with Rupert's predator's interest—the impending fate of the Sumner Redstone–controlled Viacom and CBS.

Sumner Redstone, at ninety-two, continues to control one of the choicest pools of television properties. Post-Redstone, and a parceling of assets, if not a complete breakup of the two companies—or even one of the divided companies now bidding for the other—the outcome is likely to move the market ever higher and configure new empires.

# 15

# TELEVISION WANTS TO BE PAID FOR

The American media business and, arguably, the entirety of American culture was based on the fact that television was free.

Curiously, a central aspect of the early Internet debate was the emphasis on the importance, or even moral imperative, of low-priced or no-cost information—"information wants to be free." Even though most information, or anyway most media (to make only a slight distinction), *was* free. A free Internet was hardly a disruption—instead, a continuation.

The nature of mass media, since the introduction of low-priced newspapers in the nineteenth century, was to make it as cheap as possible so that more and more people could afford it—so it could become more mass. And having mass, you could support it with advertising, which was a better economic proposition than actually trying to get people to pay the real value of information. This wasn't in fact a necessary model. Movies charged a straight user fee. So did books. Periodicals tried to balance the equation with two revenue streams, circulation and advertising. But the power of radio and then television, growing vastly larger than all other media, consigned pay content to a smaller, if not small-time, business. Even movies began to generate a great portion of their income from television sales and free-to-the-consumer distribution. Few periodicals actually covered their costs with subscription fees, and most lost money on newsstand sales.

The idea that freely provided information was a social and intellectual advance was, along with being a constant pat on the back to Internet virtue, part of the scheme to cast the Internet as a television and new mass-media model.

And yet, at the same time, in a wholly parallel world, television itself, without announcement (to a certain degree under the darkness of a complicated cable bill), was, topsy-turvy-like, converting to a paid business.

The very nature of television, of how it was received, regulated, and supported, was—far removed from the Internet—undergoing fundamental changes.

The rapid growth of cable adoption, only slightly slower (and from an infrastructure point of view vastly more complicated) than the adoption of television itself, started in the late seventies and reached critical mass penetration by the early nineties, just when consumer adoption of the Internet began. Cable's attractions had, initially, nothing to do with cable programming, but with better reception for broadcast programming—several decades of intermittent fuzz suddenly cleared. And then porn, or at least nudity, built demand (a demand that the Internet would extend and more than satisfy in coming years). And then premium channels, notably HBO, showing first-run movies and exclusive sports events. And that rather defined the universe of why people would pay for TV: better functionality, sophistication (not just sex but, as the cable programming model developed, attitudes, plots, and sensibility that you couldn't see on mere broadcast TV), exclusivity, and sports.

Later, curiously, people would pay for cable—and hence for television—in order to get Internet access, as cable companies substituted digital for the original analog signals and added broadband services.

By the time this conversion to cable was complete, it was not only the much-hated and derided cable companies that were earning fees, but all television programmers as well.

This was, as so much in television is, the result of happenstance, regulation, and negotiation.

The system that developed has cable operators paying channels, Fox News, say, or ESPN, on a per-subscriber basis.

But it was hardly intuitive that cable operators would end up paying content providers—and why should they? Cable companies were providing the one thing that channels and content makers absolutely needed: the way into people's homes, aka carriage—an audience. With access to this audience you, the content provider, could compete in this new television world and do business the old-fashioned way: you could sell ads. That was supposed to be the system.

Much like what the Internet would experience, however, it was hard to sell ads into a fractured market, against random content (early cable lacked much form or purpose), on a no-brand channel, for all that much money. It became the age of the Ginsu knife infomercial, a system in which, often, the broadcaster got paid out of a cut of the Ginsu knife sales (or not-for-sale-in-stores collections of oldie hits, or exercise videos).

The period beginning in the late seventies, and lasting ten years or so, was one in cable without fixed models, with shifting ownership of channels—for instance, HBO, ESPN, and MTV were all speculative or entrepreneurial start-ups, later sold to current owners (and largely sold because they needed further investment). It was also a period in which a new breed of television executives grew up, not so much focused on ad sales and programming, like network executives, but more focused on licensing, marketing (cable channels were niche concepts rather than mass entertainment), and a granular, deep-swamp negotiation with cable operators—a fundamental numbers game involving how to apportion existing revenues to meet everybody's existing costs.

This new breed, less focused on advertising and more focused on fees, and all out of the nascent cable industry, came to control the media business: Jeff Bewkes, CEO of Time Warner; Chase Carey, COO of 21st Century Fox; Sumner Redstone, who built Viacom; Tom Freston, who came out of MTV to run Viacom; Bob Pittman, MTV's founder, who spearheaded the rise of AOL and its merger with Time Warner, and who now runs Clear Channel; Philippe Dauman, the current CEO of Viacom; and Ted Turner, in many ways the originator of the cable programming model with CNN and the Turner Broadcasting properties.

The singular and necessary accomplishment, beyond getting a critical mass of cable companies to carry your station (for a period this resulted in a lot of ownership trade-offs—we'll carry you, if you give us an ownership stake), was to get a share of the subscription fees.

Pay channels without advertising, like HBO, paved the model—they were explicitly paid. But great—indeed viral—campaigns like "I want my MTV" created demand and enhanced negotiating positions for a channel.

Cable operators began paying Ted Turner small fees in the late seventies to get TBS when, via satellite, it was available nationally to cable stations. (Because of a quirk in the regulatory environment then, since TBS had a local broadcast license in Atlanta, it couldn't put its signal up on a satellite by itself. Instead, a third-party company did and charged that per-subscriber fee.) ESPN in 1983—when, peculiarly, it was owned by Getty Oil—started imposing larger fees.

The natural process accelerated in 1984 when Congress deregulated cable rates, which led to the expansion of tiered pricing and more aggressive fee requests from content providers.

Ultimately as cable use expanded, as cable packages grew, all boats floated, and the very concept of a cable bundle obscured costs and increased margins, meaning that, without announcement, much of television achieved—heretofore unimaginable in the television industry—a second revenue stream. As unexpected, cable fees rivaled and often exceeded advertising revenues.

The shift from advertiser-supported content to user-supported content also changed the nature of programming, shifting the traditional mass-market emphasis off a younger demographic and putting it on household members who actually made the decision to pay for an increased cable package. From here began to flower the new television golden age, programming focused on a more demanding audience—just as digital media was doing everything possible to broaden its mass base.

An inversion had occurred: digital media, which began in pay form with a pronounced aversion to advertising, had become entirely free and entirely ad supported, and television, the great advertising hellhole, the commercial Golgotha, had become strongly pay based. A discerning viewer could easily watch all the TV he or she wanted without ever seeing an ad.

# 16

# FINDING THE NEW ECONOMICS

The modern media business really did seem done for, positioning itself for a long and painful decline, and maneuvering—against the background, in the millennium's first decade, of an ever more transforming and ever more valuable digital world—for minor advantage as, relatively speaking, Rome burned.

There was clear logic to why the fire was going to consume television. And surely, many of the moves in the past decade were, on the part of the television industry, defensive or panicky ones. However, this fear forced channels to wean themselves off ad revenue. More surprisingly, as channels began to rely on fees from cable companies, those same cable companies came to control the Internet.

Viacom, in 2005, divided itself in two, one part a mostly cable programming company, retaining the Viacom name, and then the other part, a new independent CBS, a mostly network broadcaster.

Time Warner, after an assault by activist investor Carl Icahn in 2006, spun off its cable system, TWC (completed in 2009). Comcast, in 2009, bought NBC Universal, a content company.

Each of these moves suggests doubt about a fundamental direction of the business and is, in some fashion, a circling-the-wagons move.

Viacom, in part believing the Internet view that advertising will more and more migrate to digital form, pushes off CBS, its still entirely ad-supported broadcaster, in the hopes that, no longer competing with its cable channel brothers at Viacom (MTV, Comedy Central, Nickelodeon, etc.)—out to grab as much of the cable fee piece as possible—it can better negotiate with the cable system overlords.

Time Warner decides not to bet on cable's long-term future, both because of the increasing threat of over-the-top delivering of content via the Internet, and, too, because it believed cable was in a steadily weakening position in its negotiations with cable content providers (companies that it itself owns: HBO, CNN, the Turner channels).

Comcast, an amalgamation of numerous cable systems and now the biggest overlord, sees its own rather bleak future as a utility with a fast-eroding monopoly. Content gets stronger; alternative distribution gets stronger; its own technology gets weaker. What's more, it is as though it's always felt embarrassed about itself, a pipe company, far from the glamorous business it serviced. In a bungled attempt, it tried to buy Disney in 2004. Finally, in 2009, it gets GE's NBC Universal, securing its content hedge.

The effects of these television realignments play out much more discreetly than, say, the breathless rise of Facebook to its

$100 billion IPO, which also happens during this time period. And yet they are quite as transformative.

CBS's Les Moonves, that symbol of network television's lost world, turns an unexpected trick. In something of a Copernican restructuring, in 2005 he begins to put the network back at the center of the television world. The networks, once independent and dominant media entities, had all become part of vastly larger conglomerated ecosystems, vying not just with cable channels and movie and production studios, but also with the interests of the conglomerates' own local television stations. But now, with an independent CBS, Moonves controlled the network *and* the stations (heretofore an independent unit in the conglomerate) and no longer needed to heed the interests, or consider the negotiating position, of Viacom's cable channels.

In the early years, cable operators had been required to carry broadcast stations—the "must-carry rule." But in 1992, the rules changed (the Cable Television Consumer Protection and Competition Act) and broadcast stations could opt out of must-carry. This seemed like only a subtle change because obviously it was in the interest of the broadcasters to be carried by cable. But it began to open up a negotiating position. What was the point in paying for a cable bundle if it didn't carry the local CBS affiliate, say? Still, certainly for Viacom-CBS, until the split the emphasis was on cable fees, with network retrans rights thrown in as the cherry on top.

Moonves radically shifted this, effectively taking over the negotiations for his individual stations and adding the leverage of the network itself. The threat of losing a local station would not, in negotiating terms, remotely compare to the threat of losing an entire network (the cable systems had effectively gone national through a process of acquisition—so this was something of a sudden-death negotiation; either the network faced devastation without carriage, or the cable company faced devastation without one of the key broadcast networks). And within ten years these retrans fees would be a quarter of the size of total broadcast ad dollars (with syndication and foreign sales making up another quarter of the pie). In other words, Moonves had reinvented broadcast television; a lagging business became a growth industry.

Meanwhile, Time Warner, having spun off its own cable company—next to Comcast, the nation's second largest—became itself an effective pure content play. (It had already jettisoned its music company; it would soon get rid of its troubled AOL division; and it would eventually spin off its magazines.) Time Warner's essential business became its negotiation with cable operators for HBO, CNN, and the Turner channels. In a remarkable turnaround, Time Warner, which had, not long ago, nearly broken itself with a bet on a digital future, saw its cable fees rise so quickly that, in little more than half a decade following Icahn's play for the company and his call to streamline it into a pure content play, its share price had doubled (a doubling even without cable, AOL, and publishing—all spun off to the shareholders).

Comcast, for its part, found itself with its NBC Universal acquisition in an ultimate schizoid business, owning two companies whose health depended on the competition with each other. NBC Universal with its network and its cable channels needed to be wholly focused on raising the fees it derived from the cable operators, notably Comcast, hence creating a strangely zero-sum game—Comcast paid NBC, which then gave the money back to Comcast, its owner (Comcast bought out GE's remaining interest in 2013).

Now, it was possible to look at this functionally closed system as a decent hedge—Comcast wasn't going to win, but it wasn't going to lose either. It balanced the push-pull of the business.

What did confuse it, and even threaten it, was the prospect that content—including its own—might migrate to a competitive distribution system. As streaming began to grow, it became a threat—morphing from straw man to real man—in all cable negotiations: from the cable side, the specter of cord cutting was used by cable operators as leverage to hold down and hence preserve content licensing fees; from the content holders' side, the threat was that content would migrate faster to new distribution platforms without higher cable fees.

But then, in a sort of slow-motion awakening, Comcast put two and two together and began to understand that the cord could not actually be cut; or if one part of the Comcast cord was cut, another part of the Comcast cord became all the more vital.

Through a series of happenstance moves—perhaps some of the greatest happenstance in modern industrial history—cable companies had become the main provider of digital access.

In the beginning (if by beginning we mean the mid-nineties) there were two lines into most homes: twisted pair copper from the phone company, and coaxial from the cable company. Both of them highly regulated, both of them with potential to deliver broadband speeds, both of them requiring technology upgrades on the telephone and cable networks outside the home to make them able to carry broadband signals.

It turned out to be easier and cheaper at first for the phone companies to do this—first with the interim, mid-speed technology of ISDN, later with truly high-speed DSL—neither of which required particularly costly changes to implement. By 1998 DSL was being rolled out by all the Baby Bells, marketed as an upgrade over dial-up Internet service.

Meanwhile, @Home, a start-up backed by various cable operators, had launched in 1996 as the cable industry's broadband alternative to DSL. In fact, at the time, a big chunk of the local cable systems were not capable of delivering Internet service without significant investment into their networks to allow the two-way data traffic necessary for an Internet connection to function. Despite investments from TCI, Comcast, and Cox, and having co-marketing deals with most of the others (Charter, Cablevision, Rogers, etc.), @Home was at the mercy of its partners' pace of upgrades. (@Home as a company was also eventually crippled by its disastrous merger with search engine Excite in 1999, and ended up going bankrupt in 2001 in the wake of the dot-com collapse.)

The cable companies were eventually goaded into those necessary upgrades by the need to provide digital service, primarily because of competition from the expanded channel offerings of the satellite services DirecTV and Dish. Upgrading their systems to carry digital signals allowed a vast expansion of the cable dial by giving them the ability to squeeze more channels onto their network than they could with their older analog tech (and thus additional tiers of programming they could charge for), and eventually offer HDTV programming. Digital of course also finally made IP traffic possible, not to mention telephone service using voice over IP technology.

By 2002, the major cable companies were rolling out their own branded broadband services—Comcast, for example, launched Comcast High-Speed Internet that year.

The promised speeds of cable broadband were higher than DSL speeds in most markets, which was one important marketing advantage. But the real leap forward in high-speed sales for the cable industry in the mid-2000s was the introduction of bundling— offering voice, TV, and Internet at a steep discount if you took the three together. Comcast, for instance, launched its Triple Play bundle in 2005.

The phone companies were concurrently rolling out their own even higher-than-DSL-speed fiber optic services, which could offer competing bundles—Verizon FiOS, for example, launched in 2005 as well.

But the fiber installation cost was significant—as much as $750 per home—and the public markets began to balk at Verizon (FiOS) and AT&T (U-verse) making that kind of investment when those same companies were investing significant capital in building out the wireless networks they also owned. By 2010 Verizon had announced it was winding down its FiOS rollout, meaning big chunks of its coverage area wouldn't be getting it at all (Boston, for example, has never seen FiOS). They've placed their bets on the wireless business instead. (The analysts liked this because wireless pricing is essentially unregulated, whereas pricing of services over the fiber connections is subject to the state and local regulatory oversight that applies to POTS—plain old telephone service.)

Hence, Comcast, heretofore deeply worried about the future of its main business, woke up to discover that it controlled the primary way to get Internet access and, indeed, that there were few scenarios in which it could lose.

Then, in 2013, Moonves, employing both the leverage that he had amassed and his own extraordinary wiles, faced down Time

Warner Cable (that is, the cable company spun off by Time Warner, precisely in a bid to raise the leverage of content), and in a move for higher fees took CBS off the TWC system. CBS stayed dark until TWC capitulated one month later.

In part, as an effort to increase the cable leverage against content providers, and, in part, because TWC had seemed to handle itself so poorly, it almost immediately became a takeover target.

Comcast, with its new understanding that it could hold control over the two primary video distribution platforms—cable and IP—agreed to buy TWC for $45 billion. At the same time, AT&T made a deal for DirecTV.

The specter of these two deals (whether regulators permitted them to go through or not) suggested a return of video distribution back to a level of centralized control not seen since a three-network world, precipitating the great net neutrality debate, itself an opportunity not just to transform policy, but to jockey, television style, for advantage.

# 17

# NO NEUTRALS IN NET NEUTRALITY

Television is a function of government regulation. Its nature, its business, its winners and losers have largely been determined by regulators and lawmakers in an almost one-hundred-year effort to control or decontrol or change control of an expanding technology.

Imagine the existential predicament: how does government respond to a force likely to change the way people behave, think, get along with one another; a force that will redistribute and concentrate power, make favored parties rich, and sideline or bankrupt out-of-favor others?

Naturally, governments everywhere decided to regulate, most of them keeping the lion's share of television control for themselves, from direct autocratic rule to Britain's bureaucratic collective, the BBC. In the United States, the effort was to turn it over to the free market—free, of course, only in the most peculiar kind of sense. Television became an ongoing war between competing government interests, new and changing technologies, private enterprise and investor whims, national and local concerns, do-gooders and ideologues. That is, the television industry is no more a free market than the health care industry. It simply represents the struggle of good intentions, moneyed interests, transformative moments of innovation, and panicky efforts to gain control of what heretofore was overlooked and unregulated.

The structure and the spoils of digital media, on the other hand, have largely been established outside of or at arm's length from government regulation. This does not mean that there isn't an inherent regulatory structure, or that powerful interests do not exercise self-interest, or that in any way it is a more level playing field (although sometimes it might appear to be a more logical one) than the television industry. Digital media, beyond the mythology of garage start-ups, is largely a top-down business heavily influenced if not controlled by a relatively small set of investors. This group is mostly linked by a set of relationships and interests that have tended to sanction who competes with whom and even who will employ whom (e.g., the recent scandals over salary fixing and secret antipoaching agreements for tech talent).

Television and digital are hardly that different, except that one collection of interests controls one and another collection of interests controls the other.

But suddenly, at the intersection of Comcast's national broadband network, these two parallel structures—one created out of regulatory and legislative struggles, the other created out of the *keiretsu*-like favoritism and logic of finance capital—collided in a climactic battle on the issue of "net neutrality."

Except that, for most everyone involved—other than press and paid PR representatives—it was hardly win or lose. Rather, it was a complex negotiation to determine the key terms on which both sides would merge, what advantages they might preserve, and hence with what wherewithal they might continue to do battle.

The stakes are further confused by each side's negotiating advantage in misrepresenting the nature of the battle, and by the black-and-white cast of what are in fact most everyone's shaded views. But at heart, the issue had one constant: video had become the digital sine qua non. As much as 70 percent of Internet-distributed data was video, 50 percent of it from Netflix and YouTube.

Net neutrality was the Netflix issue.

But it wasn't either/or. It was not that one side wanted the net to be neutral, whatever neutral might mean, and that the other wanted to control it. Rather, both sides wanted maximum control of the distribution channel at minimum cost or maximum remuneration.

The best way to understand the Sturm und Drang of the fight was to see it not as a contest for the Internet, in itself a fairly low-bandwidth proposition, but really as a fight that had come to a high pitch because the Internet had provided a back door into the television business.

But in the telling, at least in the digital telling, it remained an elemental standoff: On one side, you had cable interests suspiciously able to influence the federal government communications bureaucracy. On the other side, you had the continuing purity of a free Internet.

But really, you had many sides not dissimilar from those that have always dogged and defined the essential muddle of communications and especially television policy:

There was the strictly pro-business side, reflecting the interests of the companies that paid for the broadband—cable operators and telcos. They naturally wanted to be able to charge bigger users higher prices.

Then there were the major Internet companies making the greatest use of the pipes. They opposed the broadband companies, both because they logically wanted to limit the leverage the pipe holders had over their own businesses, as well as to increase their leverage in their negotiations with broadband providers. Big data suppliers actually wanted better treatment, they just naturally wanted it as cheaply as they could possibly get it.

There are the Internet purists, curiously, and contradictorily, calling for more government regulation—that is, the government should enforce an unregulated Internet! (In television policy debate, the government has always been called on to regulate openness.) Otherwise, broadband providers might slow the speeds of their content competitors or even their political opponents.

There is, similarly, the opposite, pure free market position: imposing utility-like regulation, as in treating broadband like the telephone or even railroad tracks, inevitably creates a bureaucratic morass that in fact slows growth and innovation.

Then there was the position of the federal courts (in opinions that generally have a left-right consensus), which ruled in 2010 and in early 2014 that precisely because broadband is not characterized like the telephone as a common carrier, the FCC does not have the authority to mandate equal access. For it to do so, broadband would need to be reclassified as, in essence, a telephone-like system.

And recently, there's the popular culture, or populist view, most forcefully promulgated in mid-2014 by the comedian John Oliver in one of his I'm-mad-as-hell sketches on his HBO show: cable operators, like Comcast, are bad, and out to screw whomever they can screw, and all Internet users ought right away to contact the FCC and tell it how mad as hell they are. This generated a groundswell of 3 million citizen comments, most of them, presumably, against the FCC's approach, though how many of them are concerned about freedom of speech and how many of them just don't want Netflix to ever buffer remains to be seen.

And then there is the FCC itself, which, in its efforts to thread the needle in the controversy and maintain its own central position, first proposed a set of policies objectionable to pretty much everyone. While preserving various more arcane parts of net neutrality policy, it was also proposing to allow a two-tier system. While broadband providers would not be allowed to slow down traffic, they would be able to charge data providers extra to speed up their traffic. (The FCC's rules do not cover wireless, so in a sense it is a three-tier system.) But unable to find a place for itself in this new ecosystem, it then voted to designate the Internet as a utility, meaning it might be subject to as much regulation as the telephone system—guaranteeing a generation of lawsuits and further negotiation.

Arguably, we were no longer even in the Internet business, but actually in the television business, which changed the terms of the debate.

This new video industry—growing exponentially and transforming the nature of entertainment—was getting a free ride on the cable and telcos investment in broadband. This was either a) the right of the new video industry's core customers or b) unsustainable free distribution, overtaxing networks and slowing the Internet for everyone else.

Equally, this new video industry, which had grown up on the basis of free distribution, in fact wants more speed and, as well, to erect economic barriers to other Internet television upstarts. That is, in typical television policy and negotiating terms, it wants to protect and enhance its own position by creating difficult barriers for everybody else, while at the same time maintaining the best terms possible for its own account.

Nowhere was the negotiation as wily and as transparent as it was in Netflix's moves:

By the time the net neutrality debate is heatedly under way, with the Obama FCC trying to take the side of the tech community's subtly shifting positions, and the courts striking it down, it's awkwardly clear to Netflix's Reed Hastings that Netflix's great success makes it harder and harder to justify a pure net neutrality position. Netflix is consuming bandwidth at a monumental rate, vastly more than Google, even with YouTube, and for that matter everybody else.

It is also not entirely clear that net neutrality—leveled access for all—is the best situation for Netflix.

The best situation for Netflix is clearly to have as seamless a delivery as possible. Actually, the best situation is to have a more seamless delivery than its competitors. And, in a world where its most direct competitor, Amazon, is far richer and has far greater infrastructure clout, Netflix is always feeling some amount of peril.

Then, too, the logical defensive business position is to want to use its success—no matter that it was attained on the basis of a neutral net—to gain just the kind of advantages that might make it harder for someone else to do what it did. Pulling the ladder up, in other words, after you've climbed it.

Netflix commences a negotiation with Comcast that both tracks and helps establish the new FCC position. Comcast, according to prior net neutrality rules and agreements when it bought NBC, can't slow third-party data speeds, but that is not to say it can't speed them up. Hence, Comcast and Netflix develop the model for the two-speed Internet: the baseline Internet and then a faster Internet that can be bought.

Other than the downside of additional cost, Netflix has guaranteed a substantially better experience for many of its customers and, as well, it has raised the cost basis of any new movie-television-original-video-programming service that might want to compete with it.

Having established the principle of being able to buy this additional advantage, now the only ongoing issue will be the cost, a price that will be, as all things in television are, established in a negotiation wherein each side tries to establish what it has that the other wants and what it is prepared to trade in order to give it up.

Comcast, having just this sort of negotiation with the myriad channels it carries, communities that grant it franchises, and regulators whose favor it seeks, surely ought not to be surprised when an adversary sees an opportunity for additional leverage.

Netflix, filing a formal petition with the FCC, comes out against Comcast's merger with Time Warner Cable—indeed, becomes the leading antagonist to the merger in Silicon Valley—rolling it into a broad indictment of any deviation from net neutrality and of exactly the kind of two-tier deal that it had sought and accepted to safeguard and enhance its vast burden on the Comcast system.

Comcast, perhaps naively and yet reasonably, is stunned by the turnaround and betrayal, realizing quite too late that, in television fashion, Netflix not only has asserted its brand position in the television ecosystem, but could now trade back its favor and goodwill and de-escalation of righteousness, and even its ultimate acquiescence to the Comcast merger, for a better deal and, for both parties, a certain sort of television-business happiness and even "partnership" at the end of the tumult.

It is quite easy to imagine in fact an outcome in which Comcast provides Netflix, a high-speed Netflix, in its broadband bundle.

## 18

# WHEN YOUTUBE CHALLENGED TV—AND LOST

The YouTube advance, an Internet watershed moment—circa 2005—was to turn video streaming into a one-click operation. Before YouTube, Web video was a world of conflicting and often incompatible video and video players; after YouTube it was . . . television.

There was then a sea change in expectations and behavior. Internet users, emerging as though from the largely text- and photo-based Web Stone Age, expected video, and they began to behave in recognizable ways. Not only was video watched with relatively full attention (at any rate more focused attention than a fly-by Web page received), but a viewer was, mostly, forced back from the nonlinear world of the Web to having to watch from the beginning, to the middle, and even perhaps to the end. Attention, or a good piece of attention, was refocused. The Web had become, not intuitively, a narrative video medium—with sudden new entertainment format and advertising possibilities.

Reinforcing this, it became, to the growing consternation of the traditional media business, a handy way to watch actual television. Vast quantities of movies, television shows, and assorted notable video bits began to become part of, and even dominate, the YouTube library and reason for being. YouTube was on its way to being both a mega classic television network as well as a collective DVR—all television available as soon as it had aired.

Pirating, rather than cat videos, was the YouTube kick start.

The horror, to every television executive, was manifest. By the time the potential of YouTube was clear (and it very quickly became clear), the video-focused part of the media business well knew what had happened to the music part of the media business.

Music, in a shockingly short period, approximately between Napster's launch in 1999 and iTunes's launch in 2003, had escaped its owners. CD-ripping software, compressed MPEG files, and ubiquitous players liberated it. With almost no time to mount a counterattack—and, seemingly, no sentient beings in the industry to do it—the unit sales music business effectively died. The music industry sued Napster, the YouTube of music, and closed it down. But it was too late. The technology for easy ripping, compressions, and quick downloading was already widely distributed. (Briefly, the industry began to sue end users, kids in their bedrooms, deftly shifting public opinion against itself.)

The only substantial difference between music and video was the size of the digital files. It was still a burdensome process to download video—what's more, it required lots of storage space. This was a key difference, however. For one, it gave the television industry time enough to absorb the example of the music industry (in fact, television executives had always thought poorly of music executives), and to understand that the threat was existential. And, for another, it meant that YouTube became the primary and largely centralized solution for dealing with large video files—to stream rather than download.

And then YouTube was bought by Google, immediately increasing the likelihood that YouTube would be able to legitimize piracy—"sharing"—of video. (Google's practice had become to make ever more inroads into other people's content without paying—surfacing greater bits of news and other content in search results, such that a Google search page supplied a good part of the first look that anybody needed.)

Hence, YouTube became the target—a significantly more vulnerable one because Google could not, and surely would not, risk its own fortunes on a Napster-like to-the-death defense of its unprofitable YouTube division. Viacom, in the figure of octogenarian Sumner Redstone, sued it.

Curiously, from the technology side this seemed querulous and tetchy and like a sure loser. Another nuisance suit.

But it was an elemental match: YouTube was synonymous with free; Viacom makes content that needs to be paid for. And even more: digital was used to avoiding and evading direct conflict over the fundamental issues of ownership and fair use; Viacom was used to suing infringers and intellectual property adversaries.

In the media manner, bringing giant law firms and legal overkill to the process (Viacom's giant law firms and overkill necessarily matched by Google's), such contretemps became an unavoidable aspect of doing business in the space—a material issue for a public company. Viacom had injected a note (or footnote) of uncertainty into Google's future.

What's more, the suit challenged a central pillar of digital media behavior and of the digital media business: the Digital Millennium Copyright Act (DMCA).

This 1998 piece of legislation, passed in the first flush of digital enthusiasm and soaring share prices (prior to the 2000–2002 dot-com crash), provided in some real sense safe harbor to infringers. If an infringer acts reasonably within a short period of time—that is, by expunging and taking down the copyrighted material—he stays in good order and faces no penalties (vastly different from the standards in traditional media, where any infringement can involve substantial damages and awards). In practice this afforded an infringer a very low bar. The burden was put on the copyright holder to monitor and police its material and then give notice to the offender, at no peril, to take it down—in other words, a one-sided statute to the clear disadvantage of owners of premium content. By filing a big lawsuit, backed by bottomless legal resources (which no other media organization had yet the temerity or uncoolness to do), Viacom was issuing a very high-level warning that the DMCA and YouTube's use of it to maintain an effective structure of piracy, one without penalties to itself, wouldn't be tolerated without a fight.

In a sense, too, it was a particular kind of litigation: an ever-present threat to its public company adversary. Lawsuits are not necessarily always about disposition, but frequently about the symbolic meaning of the threat of constant litigation, bad will, querulous and noisome press, and moral and political one-upmanship.

The long and grinding suit was probably at best a draw, and

involved a series of setbacks before the settlement for Viacom—allowing the digital side to wave it away as more ineffectuality on the part of the old in its competition with the new. But during the suit, and arguably—a strong argument—because of the suit, the weather entirely changed. Google and YouTube became an effective (if begrudging) self-policer and fundamentally shifted out of the piracy business into user-generated content and, more important, into a set of agreements with content makers. Instead of a common carrier they had become, in a major transformation, licensors.

If video piracy was not defeated, it was—to a large degree the result of the Viacom suit—pushed back to the margins. Digital media wasn't stealing television's business; it was entering it.

# 19

# YOUTUBE BECOMES NOT *YOU*TUBE

YouTube was not conceived as television. It was conceived in one of those digital conceptual cones such that if it had been explained to you without its real-world demonstration and adoption—you'll be able to instantly see random home videos that can be uploaded by anybody (but no porn)—you would have likely been stumped by the usefulness of it to anyone.

Its development into a near-universal compendium of video promotions, self-consciousness, and personal entrepreneurial gestures was a happenstance outcome that could hardly have been anticipated, or, except as a document of human theatrical nature, its vast server resources justified.

Google bought it in 2006, not because it saw value in it as a going business concern, but as a new instance of human behavior. And that's what Google does: centralize such instances, and then monetize the compulsive behavior.

There was certainly no admission, or evidence, that Google thought it was going into the television business when it bought YouTube.

Rather, it was an extension of the search business, a vast collection of information that might yield further information about the interests and habits and inclinations and desires of the people searching it. Against this marketing mother lode, Google figured it ought to be able to take its usually handsome vig.

Again, nobody at Google saw this as show business.

And, with the Viacom lawsuit, it saw the perils of stepping on show business toes. Show business, rather unlike the information business, litigated ferociously.

And yet, there really ought to have been a threshold understanding: Video, no matter how truncated, or "real," or the work of amateurs, is, at least to the market, performance and story. It was not going to be monetized as a mere function of data or compulsive behaviors. (In fact, to the extent it was, it seemed to show the low value of such a strategy—prices going down, not up.) It needed to be monetized for its impact—its message, its resonance, its characters and stories. If it could not be, then it seemed awfully likely it was going to stay a bizarre morass of sideshow content.

In other words, YouTube was, whether Google liked it or not, on a long, circuitous, even quite tortured, journey into television.

In that regard, it began to be clear that the main YouTube executive job was to undo what it was and turn it into what it might profitably be. This ended up creating a weird hearts-and-minds schism. YouTube, at least from the point of view of market logic, had to be the opposite of YouTube.

It was something of the digital media paradigm: technology

had enabled a substantially new notion of behavior and expression that, if it was going to offer a decent return, was going to have to look and act a lot more like the old notion of behavior and expression.

The YouTube experience could not spell out media reality more clearly, a message sent to the rest of the digital media industry: video was television and the television business worked in very fixed ways. For one thing, it was not a random, or long-tail, experience. In television the valuable rose to the top. What's more, that "top," to realize ultimate value, had to conform to some brand's usually quite conservative idea of cultural norms.

YouTube, wholly advertising supported, was not just in the television business, it was in the old-fashioned, wholly sponsor-dependent, television business.

Within YouTube itself this became a difficult and contentious notion. On the one side, there was represented the spirit of the medium, idiosyncratic and anarchic, attracting the worldwide devotion of video hobbyists and self-promoters, but unable to adequately monetize itself. On the other side, there was a new Google-imposed discipline that said that YouTube had to conform to the desires of the video advertising market but, creating further message confusion, this side, coming from digital media, knew little about the actual working of the video advertising market—in other words, television.

A not-unexpected logic and plan unfolded. Google, starting in 2011, would turn to the professional television production industry to help it create more professional and marketable YouTube fare—or channels.

Google money suddenly fueled a video production boomlet

(one that in turn would spur the growth, and competitive furor, of digital video everywhere else on the Web). It was, briefly, silly money or dumb money. Google itself, as though to reinforce the etherealness or lack-of-stakes or get-it-while-you-can aspect, kept calling this an experiment.

Soon enough, albeit hundreds of millions of dollars later, it revealed itself to be a failed experiment. Its results were not just bad, they were utterly perplexing. Professional television producers making YouTube-like television were not nearly as successful in attracting viewers as YouTube amateurs—and in neither instance were advertisers very impressed.

Abandoning this experiment, YouTube refocused its efforts on its own homegrown stars and producers. There was, around YouTube videos, a growing professional culture. There were large, convention-type gatherings of YouTube performers and promoters. Hollywood talent agencies, keen to have digital bona fides, had YouTube-focused agents. Maker Studios, a native producer of YouTube videos and promoter of YouTube talent, was sold to Disney for more than $500 million.

YouTube, suddenly excited that YouTube might finally be catching up with the market, launched a major campaign—much of it in old media—to promote, in television fashion, its own stars.

Google sent in one of its key executives, Susan Wojcicki, who had masterminded much of Google's search advertising strategy. Wojcicki said the YouTube strategy was to be more like television.

In essence, it was a bifurcated strategy. The original YouTube would be relegated to a nether YouTube, a low-end and low-margin outlet, like certain low-performing areas of the cable dial. A new, sanctioned, and promoted YouTube, with content more suitable and tailored to big advertising brands, would rise to the top and become the face of YouTube. It even had a name, YouTube Preferred. Wojcicki explicitly articulated the new, adult, profit-potential You-Tube rationale in an Orwellian language reminiscent of 1970s network television: "It works for advertisers, but it also works for creators. It gets back to this ecosystem issue. If you are a top creator, you want to make sure that you are in front of the brand advertisers who want to spend more dollars on the platform. And if you are an advertiser you actually want to also be with the creators who are going to complement your advertising messages."

If you can cut through the corporatese, what you see is an executive trying to stick a finger in the dike of falling ad revenues. The exact process everyone else is working to erode—with all traffic becoming equal and divided by calculable demographics rather than ranked by tastes—is the television world YouTube is hoping to recreate.

Television was YouTube's business, but one—perhaps because Wojcicki and the rest of Google's management were in temperament and craft remote from it—that it was a long way from cracking.

An analyst at the investment bank RBC Capital Markets, David Bank, summed up the dynamic and Google's quandary in late 2014: an entire week of YouTube is roughly as valuable to major advertisers as a single, first-run episode of *The Big Bang Theory*.

Wojcicki's view of the business seemed a little like battlefield triage. Television, however inadvertently it had come to YouTube, was the hand it had to play. If this involved a subscription plan, so be it. If this involved licensing premium video content, that, too, was a viable option—that, in other words, YouTube might be Net-flix. What seemed clear is that the future of YouTube was not You-Tube. It was the established video marketplace.

# 20

# FACEBOOK TELEVISION

Curiously, while the Facebook News Feed was once an effort to create a new information experience, each friend a provider or filterer of necessarily personalized information, the effort, more and more, has been to focus, sharpen, and limit the News Feed in ways that are much more reminiscent of traditional media than of the flattened, random information landscape of the Web.

Reasonably, as the Facebook News Feed goes, so goes digital media.

In 2014, Facebook, heretofore reliant on embedded clips from YouTube and other platforms, launched its own video player—like television itself, the video is running as you enter.

Mark Zuckerberg's notion of a mostly video News Feed is both obvious and disingenuous. Digital media is more and more image based; an increasing proportion of those images are video; video is now trivial to make and upload; Facebook's player, as well as many others, makes it seamless to watch; video offers many more "premium" advertising opportunities than text. What's not to like?

But in another way it is an entire remaking of Facebook, a remaking that offers any number of ultimately divergent outcomes, starting with the question of how much you want to be in the social media business or how much you might rather be in the television business—or which is more dominant when you try to marry the two.

Asked another way: is the move into video guided more by advertising and revenue growth, or by Facebook's notions of social stimuli and changing modes of behavior? (Both, they will say, of course, but if only for argument's sake, choose one.)

In a sense, Facebook video seems inevitably and merely to be YouTube—and, at that, YouTube of four years ago—with your friends using Facebook to showcase their personal and promotional videos. This may be the natural water level of the form: transient, low-value, shared media keepsakes (keepsakes nobody keeps). And, anyway, in a sense the form, and its inherent value (or lack of value), may hardly matter. The greater point is the competition between the two ruling digital media platforms: Facebook and Google/YouTube. Basic platform theory is that dominance will win you the future (even if the shape and strategy of the future is unclear). Hence, Facebook, the upstart, tries to steal market share and ad dollars from Google in as many categories as possible, launching products like search and now video to do so. In other words, the choice between social media business or television business is a faulty one; rather, it's a consistent effort to achieve dominance in the platform business.

On the other hand, it's still video, a demanding and expensive form.

As the value of amateur video sinks, the hope at YouTube, and now, too, at Facebook, is in "premium video."

It is worth a moment to consider just what premium video is: It is the opposite of native Internet video. It is not that it is better, but it has a clearer provenance; it has a brand; it is produced, according to Facebook, by a publisher. This in itself is odd, because publishers publish, they don't produce (true, the act of publishing has taken on some highly attenuated metaphorical meaning in digital media; nevertheless, it still means what it means). But the premise here is that video has become so artless to produce that anybody can do it, including publishers without particular video expertise, but who nevertheless have a brand authority. Hence, Time Inc. became the first publisher to upload videos to the Facebook video player. Now it is worth noting that Time Inc. was spun off from Time Warner precisely because it was not in the video or television business. And that rather is an indication of Facebook's level of video play: it's reliant on a new, low-level entrant in video, albeit with a well-known name, though not one in video. That's premium. A code word for second-rate, but openly better than third-rate. (Also worth noting, Time Inc. was the first mainstream contributor to AOL, helping it vault from message board to media—to ultimate calamity.)

But premium is relative, of course. Today's premium easily becomes tomorrow's dross. The competition among publishers with no particular expertise in making videos is already resulting in a glut of underproduced, underwritten, underpresented, more or less desperate-feeling videos from heretofore quality-conscious brands. Hence, soon enough, the game will kick up a notch—and then another.

The point is that premium means better than the average, whereas Facebook's basic business has all been based on the average, on the glut, on the dross—it didn't matter what people posted as long as they posted a lot.

Premium changes that. It requires the act and the process of distinguishing your product. It means you have to economically incentivize the makers of your product to do more—in other words, the price goes up.

What you are doing is moving out of that strictly Internet form, one-to-one, nonhierarchical, no filter, come as you are, into the opposite form, which is produced, selected, sanctioned, curated. Yuri Milner's idea that, in social media, you don't have to pay for content is, in other words, wholly disrupted. The Internet ethos of unmediated conversation and contribution is cast aside if not obsoleted.

Facebook is, too, in its premium efforts and in its market share war with Google and YouTube, trying to attract YouTube stars into its own News Feed firmament. This represents a curious homogenization. It also sets up something of an inevitable bidding war. The economic model for acquiring entertainment product in digital media becomes no different from the model in traditional media. Facebook and Google are merely competing networks. (CBS was the fledgling network in the mid-1950s until Bill Paley stole much of NBC's talent.)

And likely, in the hunt for limited top-of-the-top premium content (i.e., proven hits), Facebook and Google both become competitors and collaborators with traditional networks and producers, reestablishing the offline pattern of networks fighting for ratings but at the same time, through syndication and other production deals, selling one another's products.

On the one hand, in its sales pitches for video ads, Facebook is touting its ability to steal ad dollars from network and cable TV (this is from a purloined Facebook sales deck that made the rounds):

1. You want to be where people are. Changing consumer behavior should shape where you spend your marketing dollars.
2. You want to reach all of the people who matter to you. Facebook has unparalleled targeted reach.
3. You want to be in the most engaging digital real estate, which, as you just saw, is Facebook's News Feed.

*Forbes*, echoing Facebook's pitch and, as well, the twenty-year promise of digital media, intoned in its coverage of Facebook's new sales initiative: "TV networks, Facebook is coming for your business. Don't say they didn't warn you."

But at the same time, Facebook was playing up its value as a TV partner. It sees itself as the perfect promoter for television shows, being able to combine previous "likes" of similar shows, and intersecting friends' likes with your likes in some hit-making data wonder. The next step seems as natural: Facebook, in Netflix, Hulu, or Amazon fashion (but, as possibly, in combination with Netflix, Hulu, or Amazon and with all other producers and distributors), becomes an OTT bundler delivering video streams within its platform. See an ad for *How to Get Away with Murder* on Facebook, then, with a new pay-TV authentication function, you can click to watch it via the appropriate app on the device of your choice.

In other words, Facebook sees itself as a potential new sort of dial, serving up television recommendations from your friends as well as through paid promotions, all seamlessly toggled to your existing accounts or credit card info for single-episode purchases.

In the digital worldview, this remains an example of the coming and inevitable disruption of the old media world, but that's just a continuing solipsism. Facebook might now still exist in something of an independent world of its own making, but in a world of exclusivity and of ultimate premium content, leverage is at best divided between producer and distributor, between buyer and seller, and invariably tipping toward the hit maker.

# PART 5

# THE NEW TELEVISION—OR THE NEW OLD TELEVISION

# 21

# PREMIUM PLUS PLUS PLUS

Everyone was, in their way, suddenly in the television business, albeit mostly the cheap television business. *The New York Times*, which, in sixty years of coexistence with television, had not confused what it did with what television did, or presumed that it could do what television did, was suddenly an aggressive video producer. Every reporter who hoped to go anywhere at *The New York Times* had to be able to produce video and to be a video star, to turn his or her own maladroitness, bad wardrobes, and ungainly features into some kind of charming shtick.

In some sense the perception was, digital allows us the freedom to produce bad (and low-cost) content.

That seemed to be one of the fundamental new media advances: low content costs. Produce so much content at such low costs that no one would quite notice it was dross. At least, they wouldn't feel like they could complain.

Indeed, Google, Facebook, and Twitter, along with most other digital publishing platforms, have had virtually no content costs.

The premise has been that technology itself—functionality—provided the media's reason for being. Users and the new tools available to them would create the interest and frisson and habituation that would propel the medium—and give it an unbeatable cost advantage over traditional media.

Even content-specific sites have largely and rigorously held to this new spend-less standard: a smaller revenue base simply means a smaller budget. (A continuing and perhaps insuperable conundrum for traditional media trying to adopt a digital form is the transition of costs. *The New York Times*'s digital product—what it says is its future—would be impossible without the content provided by and paid for by its paper.) An argument has been that, along with user-generated content—a kind of economic digital media grail for the past several years—digital tools and conventions can create a much lower content cost basis than has existed in traditional media.

One key aspect of this has been aggregation, a constant reprocessing and redistribution and ultimate universal sharing of the same material, with its attendant effect of sameness and brand dilution and lower value.

Part of the effort to break out of that downward spiral has been the wide adoption of original video. But this, too, was looked at in low-cost digital terms. Here was the possibility of a unique product, one that commanded significantly higher advertising fees, but that was yet cheap to make. A revolution in camera and editing technology had reduced the basic cost of production to practically nothing. And YouTube had established a set of production-value conventions that even seemed to make more expensive television conventions largely irrelevant—even a negative.

It was cheap, but it was video. Hence, a step up. Premium content.

In effect, the assumption was that this new kind of video— cheap, on-the-fly, guerrilla, anybody-can-do-it video—was a new form. Many of the advantages of television without most of the costs.

Suddenly, there was a new sort of video maker, multichannel networks, essentially professional video makers imitating, as yet unprofitably, amateur video makers in order to attract YouTube traffic. (Several have been bought by established studios, not so much for their moneymaking capabilities as for their ability to seed YouTube with promotional videos for the studios' real productions.)

But success here (success such as it is) repeated the digital paradigm: every low-entry-hurdle advance is, in short order, adopted everywhere in digital media.

While the advertising rates for this new premium product were higher than the price of the nonpremium general Web page product (ever continuing to fall), in short order the price of the premium product now glutting the market began to fall too.

Hence, naturally, there became a market demand for what was inevitably called "premium plus." That is, better, more original, higher production quality video.

In some sense, digital media had morphed from its newspaper stage—*The Dacron Republican-Democrat*—into an early-cable-like phase (with a strong "public access" aura), a new world of low-cost video.

And, similarly, the digital media hope, or assumption, was that it would now do to cable what it did to newspapers—it would democratize video, free it.

But among the differences, newspapers had been a diminishing form for many years, with little investment or improvement, and digital media brought innovations in search and speed and access, if not quality. Cable, on the other hand, had been continually upgrading its product, to the point where its own large margins were under pressure from constant new production upgrades and higher budget thresholds. What's more, it was unclear what technology, beyond streaming (television's most basic functionality, with performance standards still significantly ahead of digital), actually brought to video. Other than there being vastly more of it (arguably a drawback as much as an advance), digital technology did not really enhance or change the experience of video—neither for the audience nor for the advertiser. Arguably it diminished the experience: lower quality and more awkward advertising integration (preroll was easy to avoid).

Still, as though a promised land, almost everywhere digital media was turning itself into a cable-like business, but a lesser cable-like business (if cable was once lesser than broadcast, digital was now lesser than cable), and, of course, with more of it.

One reasonable way of reading this is to see digital not on a hopeless path, but instead on a well-trod one.

Cable began largely as the creation of infrastructure companies and then yielded, or its programming yielded, for better or worse, to entertainment companies.

The laughable, low-rent, kind-of-quaint sensibility of cable's first ten years yielded first to broadcast television's cast-off and lower-earning properties, building an extraordinary new market for them (e.g., classic TV), and then, almost always under the tutelage of experienced programmers, into a recognizable but distinct television form.

And, obviously, this is what is happening at Netflix, Amazon, Yahoo, and Google and Facebook to come. Media is an ever-tiered business in which you rise up, often at your peril, from the ordinary and amateur to the more proficient to, sometimes, the unique and original, and on to the slick and professional and then to the search for the one-of-a-kind, perfectly realized franchise.

In this, digital becomes a video programming platform with more similarities to than differences from all other video programming platforms, partly a new competitor in the business, but also simply an expansion of it, highly reliant on the existing video product and talent pool.

# 22

# REPACKING THE UNBUNDLE

For every direction, no matter how strong, there is the potential, even inevitability, of the opposite direction.

That is, in this instance, "unbundling." Remember that television viewers rarely rise up en masse for anything, but a true groundswell has pushed HBO to offer their HBO GO service without having to have cable. Now that HBO has agreed to that, and ESPN has a package for cord cutters, the question has primarily become: who will be next?

Bundling is, from the digital perspective, what's wrong with media. And digital's à la carte model is the historical inevitability that will defeat big media.

In a bundled system you need to buy everything to get the select pieces that you want—that is, you're forced to pay for what you don't want (you may not watch sports, but you're paying for them, boy are you paying for them, anyway). À la carte is the freedom to choose, and pay for, only what you want.

The à la carte impulse is, in digital-speak, the motor of piracy, which has been the undoing of the music industry. Why pay for an entire CD when you just want one song? Such a new model, or freedom, has equally undone the print industry: newspaper and magazine articles now float freely and can be selected independently from the whole. Why pay for the whole *New York Times* when you just want one article—a reading approach that undermines the paper's ability to spread its costs and to create a whole.

That last is the traditional media response: be careful what you wish for.

Bundling is the rational economic model for, in the end, providing you with more of what you want. Forcing the consumer to pay for, in effect, a blind pool of content (i.e., you really don't know what you're going to get) is a way to finance the new and untested, the mid-range, the worthy, the experimental, the duds, from which, of course, the hits arise. But if you just sell the hits, you can't have the other stuff, which, in turn, will affect the quality of the hits. In a sense, Hollywood movies have become something of an unbundled world. Instead of a wide and serendipitous selection, it is a world of predictable patterns: sequels, remakes, and franchise films (what studios know the market wants).

The *new* new golden age of television has happened because there is no precise accounting. AMC can produce *Mad Men* because AMC is part of the cable package, whether you watch *Mad Men* or not (and, relatively speaking, not many people do).

Of course we live in an ever more hit-driven world, and that

same demand for hits gives packagers the leverage to sell
bundles—but it also strains the logic of the system. Why can't I
have only what I want?

And not only is the system hard to rationalize, it is, for the
bundlers, easy to take advantage of. Cable fees hover at what not
that long ago would have been unimaginable levels because your
need for one thing allows them to blackmail you into paying for it
all. What choice do you have?

Digital says you do, and you should.

Little occupies the minds of many television executives so
much as this threat.

Not long ago, I arrived for breakfast with one of the most famous agents in the world—his third, or fourth, or tenth breakfast
no doubt. As I approached, I saw he was with a recognizable, indeed iconic figure—and I hesitated, self-consciously watching
Whoopi Goldberg take a sip of juice.

"Whoopi," said the agent, "you know Michael."

She rose with a kind of royal resignation and, not knowing me
from Adam, said, "Yes, so well," and took what she immediately
understood was her cue to go.

I replaced her at the table and the agent, leaning in, said of the
increasingly past-her-prime star: "She is so fucked in an à la carte
world."

Except that as much as it is a threat—pursued to its logical end
like music, a few people make big sums, the rest of the industry
takes scraps—it is a puzzle.

Between the bulwark and the apocalypse—putting aside the
fate of the music industry—there ought yet to be a lot of room to
maneuver.

And if there is a fundamental television talent, beyond popular narrative technique, it is maneuvering for advantage.

The digital side tends to see it, or at least cast it, not only as a music-like overthrow, but as a music-like certainty.

But unbundling of music—wherein a great many consumers became accustomed to single-song choice in a very short period of time and, as though overnight, a single-song system was effectively put in place—caught everybody unaware. The television bundle, on the other hand, is a tendentiously debated affair.

In addition to the digital position, there is the political one, driven by complaints about rising cable bills, which has raised the interest in unbundling. Everybody hating their cable operator makes them a safe target for mau-mauing by politicians—you don't lose many votes when you do it. This leads to things like John McCain's introduction of legislation in 2013 to force unbundling, as well as the FCC's recent me-too interest in the topic.

In a straight-up world, the prospect of more oversight and more regulation might otherwise be worrisome to an industry. But the unbundling debate tends to reduce to a cable-digital divide.

There's cable on one side, with its opaque packages and high fees; digital, on the other, with its promise of vast à la carte menus, but inevitably under the thumb and designs of secretive and hegemonic platforms. And, as a vastly interested third party, the producers of content, who benefit from bundling, depend on it even, but who benefit, in some cases with greater advantages, from many unbundling scenarios.

In some sense, everybody is looking for leverage in their negotiations with cable (and satellite) providers: the digital players for greater speed at lower cost into the home; producers for great fees from content distributors (e.g., cable and satellite, but ultimately any distributors, including digital platforms). Political leverage can offer a real negotiating threat. On the other hand, it is in a sense home turf for the cable industry and particularly Comcast. A legislative and regulatory battle results, one might say with vast assurance, not in unbundling but in a renegotiation of the bundle—with, in the end, the advantages won or lost being unclear for years to come. (Already, FCC chairman Tom Wheeler is proposing that various OTT services be classified as multichannel video programming distributors—"MVPD"—meaning instead of being the new freewheeling à la carte providers, they'll be subject to regulation too—meaning not only pushback from cable, but pushback from digital platforms.)

What's more, if the à la carte argument seems to have captured the high-road logic—why pay for what you don't consume—the virtuous bundling argument is, more and more, being cogently spun. There are the extreme arguments that suggest nothing less than an entire breakdown of the video entertainment system, with one analyst, Laura Martin, at Needham & Company, doing an apocalyptic math that put something like $100 billion at risk—an I-dare-you-to-meddle form of argument to regulators. And then, for regulators, there is the perhaps more worrisome argument that changes in the television ecology might well make prices for the consumer go up rather than down, that not only will choice decline, but the aggregate cost for the consumer to assemble the content he or she wants will be more than the current package now. "For households filled with people of differing tastes or fans of many channels, this future could make the average cable TV bill—which hovers at around $90—seem like a bargain," noted *The Wall Street Journal*.

This is valid on some more and more obvious levels. The video world is unbundling and we can see some of the effects: at this point, more choice, but more fees. OTT offerings are in effect channels we're adding to the cable bundle—the suggestion is that they are premium channels like HBO, but that is really not quite true. Netflix isn't HBO right now, it's AMC or TNT: a basic cable channel with a couple of headline prime-time shows backed by a library of rerun movies and TV series. The question is, how many of those separate (but really the same) services will you be willing to pay for? All of them mixing and remixing bits and pieces of the same library content.

The underlying argument here is that the system is too complex, interdependent, and fraught for any sane person to want to mess with—the center holds because, if not strong, it is the devil you know.

What's more, the threats of unpredictable ecosystem disruption are also directed by cable companies against programmers—that is, cable systems themselves threaten to unbundle as leverage against programmers seeking higher fees.

On the other hand, if it does shake out this way—vastly more segmented outlets—the potential opportunity here for the programmers is to create even more syndication outlets for their libraries, beyond what they have with the existing universe of traditional channels. Syndication, of course, became a much more lucrative business for owners of content libraries when the video world expanded from a handful of channels in broadcast to the one-hundred-plus-channel world of cable. Syndication in an unbundled OTT world might likely add greater levels to the three-dimensional chess game of pricing strategies and exclusivity windows for library content, as well as original programming.

There is, too, in any discussion of the merits and inevitability of OTT choice versus the cable bundle the still incontestable virtues of the traditional infrastructure. At least in the near term, it remains a more reliable delivery mechanism for video—no network slow-downs that lead to stalled streams and spinning balls in the middle of your screen. In fact, in an unbundled world it's possible to imagine the "old" tech (current TV) actually being marketed more as a "premium" service to consumers—in the way, in fact, that cable was originally marketed, as technology that gave you, finally, a reliably clear picture.

Ironic that while there's this discussion about programming being unbundled, the pathways through which consumers access this stuff are available at a heavy discount only if bought in a bundle of phone/Internet/TV from the telcos and cable operators. Theoretically these are all available to you unbundled, but at a much higher price if you tried to buy them separately—or exactly what the doomsayers are predicting will happen in an unbundled TV world. But it's also an indication that the moment unbundling becomes official, we'll get offers on rebundled packages of programming that will be significantly cheaper than buying à la carte.

Unbundling is more accurately rebundling—sometimes in a more efficient way but, of course, efficient bundles tend sooner or later to become inefficient.

FiOS, Verizon's broadband service, is now bundling Netflix, along with HBO, Showtime, basic cable, and broadcast, into its Internet access package for $60 a month, whereas, on its own, Netflix costs $9 a month.

It is easy to imagine in the OTT world of rebundling a far larger variety of bundle options than we currently get from our cable/sat providers—things like a twenty-five-channels-for-$25 option, where you get one or two premium channels that you really want bundled with the twenty-three collections of dreck. This is essentially what the programmers do already in their negotiations with the operators, forcing them to take their secondary channels, which they charge pennies per sub for, if they want to buy AMC or ESPN. It would just be applied more transparently to the consumer.

But it is still bundling.

# PART 6

# CONTENT IS KING—WELL, IT IS ON TELEVISION

# 23

# SINE QUA NON

If digital wants to steal TV's business, especially its big brand advertising, why are there no sports?

Why not, in television style, bid for exclusive rights to stream a sporting event and thereby draw exactly those high-margin brand advertisers who so far have largely disdained digital media and kept it in the shadow of television?

In fact, in the summer of 2013, shortly before the NFL's billion-dollar Sunday Ticket deal with DirecTV was due to expire, Google and YouTube executives met with the NFL, as, many assumed, a prelude to bidding on the package. But the new price went to $1.4 billion, and Google retreated without making a formal offer.

It may just be that digital media moguls and entrepreneurs continue to hope digital media will somehow find another avenue before making the ultimate programming bet. Or it may just reflect an aspect of the small-time in digital media moguls and entrepreneurs. Digital media is mere retail banking, and sports is a high-risk and arcane financial instrument, requiring television's cleverer and more cutthroat schemers.

At any rate, there is no television without sports. As certainly, there is no sports, at least no mega–sports media complex, without television. This is a partnership on the level of gas and cars.

Similarly, there may be no way to compete with television without sports.

Sports is the purest media construct—the original and ultimate reality television. It's news with a real-time cliff-hanger outcome. We know something is going to happen, we know when, and we know who is involved, but we don't know what—and there is a built-in, obsessive audience that passionately wants to know.

It's all in the marketing handbook—or the marketing handbook was written on the basis of the easy byplay between brands and sports:

The sports industry's ability to generate popular live events has been invaluable to brand advertisers for decades, not only for their built-in commercial breaks, but for their seemingly endless inventory of in-event sponsor mentions, which began in more commercially innocent times but which persist to this day: while boomer Yankee fans fondly remember Mel Allen's incorporation of "Ballantine Blasts" and "White Owl Wallops" into his calls of Mickey Mantle home runs on radio and television in the fifties and early sixties, their children and grandchildren have grown accustomed to seeing NFL field goals and extra points brought to them by the Good Hands of Allstate.

That importance to brands has only advanced as consumers have gained an ever-increasing ability to time-shift and fast-forward through commercial breaks in other forms of programming. Even with efforts to insert unskippable ads into shows, the overall trend appears to be working inexorably against advertisers. Sports, however, exists only in real time—the ads are part of life, and, by this time, part of the sports experience and general bonhomie.

The fact that sports continues to have unique and obsessive appeal to young male consumers, a holy grail often difficult for advertisers to reach through other means and media, is another factor in its extraordinary commercial and cultural value. In fact, sports, with its communal and must-see focus, has become more important to advertisers even while audiences for individual events have declined. (The World Series once commanded staggering ratings: the seventh game of the 1986 Series between the Red Sox and Mets, for example, drew a 38.9 Nielsen rating. In the 2014 Series between the San Francisco Giants and Kansas City Royals, the comparable seventh game drew a 13.7/23—and yet the 2014 Series was yet another advertising bonanza, yielding Fox $520,000 for each thirty-second spot. The Super Bowl remains the exception to general fracturing, with 2014's game drawing a 46.7 rating, not far off the all-time high of a 49.1/73 in 1982.)

Mass-market sports has been, in large part, a three-network (with Fox coming later) phenomenon, the result not just of marketing kismet, but of the highest levels of showmanship. Roone Arledge, who ran ABC Sports and then ABC News, fundamentally reshaped television and American sports as well by using exclusive access and high production values in televising sports as the ultimate competitive advantage in the ratings wars.

It is, too, a deal game, about long, labyrinthine relationships that, like all of television, doubled down on complexity with the growth of cable's parallel television culture and even more byzantine deal structures.

The sports-cable relationship goes back to the late sixties, when Cablevision launched what eventually became the Madison Square Garden Network, the model for future regional sports networks (RSNs). Professional sports teams had traditionally relied on ticket sales as their major source of revenue. During the broadcast heyday, the sports leagues had actually restricted the number of games they licensed for broadcast, figuring that too much inventory on TV would cut into the sale of game tickets.

But the growth of cable and the expansion of regional networks in the eighties changed the revenue mix for sports. RSNs and the carriage fees they charged to cable operators—a large percentage of which was passed through to the teams as the rights holders—became increasingly lucrative, and more game inventory moved to television. Where teams and leagues had once enforced a deliberate scarcity, it's now rare if any professional game in the major sports (baseball, football, basketball, and hockey)— and most of the top college games—is *not* televised in some form. Because of local political pressure for games to remain on "free" TV, some franchises (the Yankees and Mets, for example) still show a limited selection of games on over-the-air broadcast affiliates in their local markets. But in most markets, a full or nearly full schedule of each pro sports team's games appears on cable.

At the same time that RSNs were on the rise in the eighties, national cable sports was undergoing a revolution with the creation and growth of ESPN, which in its earliest years charged nothing for carriage, and is now far and away the most expensive cable channel per subscriber.

ESPN's success for Disney has led its broadcast competitors—CBS, Fox, and NBC—to all launch their own national sports networks, although none of them yet has the carriage or breadth of rights to challenge ESPN in viewer numbers or deal negotiations. But the arrival of these networks is putting upward pressure on rights fees. When ESPN extended its deal with the NFL in 2011 for *Monday Night Football*, for example, it agreed to pay $15.1 billion over eight years. The sports leagues themselves have also gotten into the national cable network game, with the NFL, MLB, and NBA all launching their own networks in recent years, and now even college conferences like the SEC, Big Ten, and Pac-12 have launched their own networks.

The major media companies have also become big players in the RSN business, bidding on local cable rights in multiple markets. Comcast, for example, has RSNs in fourteen markets, including the San Francisco Bay Area, Chicago, Philadelphia, and New York. Fox currently has more than twenty RSNs, including ones in Los Angeles and New York, where it recently bought a controlling interest in the YES Network from the Yankees.

One major factor in their success over the years has been their inclusion as part of basic cable packages—the RSNs themselves obviously wanting to negotiate for this in order to increase their ad rate base, and the cable companies, at least in the early years, agreeing to it because having the games helped to lure customers. Only recently have the rising per-subscriber fees for RSNs caused system operators to begin balking at the cost. In Los Angeles, the Dodgers and Time Warner Cable partnered to launch SportsNet LA in early 2014, a twenty-five-year deal paying the Dodgers more than $8 billion. (A huge sore spot in southern California, where many fans can no longer watch the Dodger games because it's not part of their cable package.) The Dodgers' ownership of the network is the latest in a trend of team ownership of partial or full stakes in the RSNs, which began as early as 1984, when the Red Sox ownership group at the time launched the New England Sports Network, originally as a premium service. The biggest financial force in professional baseball has gone from having a new stadium to having a new local cable deal. The reason for the Oakland Athletics' continuing with a "Moneyball" strategy comes less from their aging stadium than from their disastrous TV deal signed in 2009. Rumored to be for less than half a billion dollars over twenty-five years, signed before the big RSN explosion, the deal gives them far less cash to work with than their peers, and for decades to come.

The $4 or more per subscriber SportsNet was seeking was among the highest fees for any RSN, despite the fact that the network carried the games of just one team (most RSNs have at least two—baseball and basketball, or baseball and hockey, for example—so they can offer live programming throughout most of the year).

For major digital platforms, most long resistant to paying for content—and at this point accustomed to not paying for it—there must be something otherworldly about looking at the sports market. Sports might even be the steepest, most fearsome, most slippery slope. If you start to pay copiously here, then why not somewhere else? Google, for instance, in its aggressive use, without fees, of news content in search results—how do you justify paying one content provider nothing, and another vast sums?

Of all the cultural conflicts between digital media and traditional media, sports might be the most extreme. Beyond the cost and deal complexities (sixty years' worth of those byzantine and lucrative deal structures), there are the generations of relation-ships, many on the local level, between teams, leagues, owners, and the sports media establishment—among the most dramatic and fraught examples of media as a one-to-one salesmen's game, an old-boys' club, and a serious, impenetrable business cabal.

But without sports—as it is without beginning, middle, and end narrative—it is hard, perhaps impossible, to be in the pre-mium media business. But with sports—and this might be the ultimate rub—you really do begin to exit the form and function of the digital media business. You not only turn your cost structure on its head, but you commit yourself to a way of doing business, and a reason for doing business, that has very little to do with technology.

Sports is showmanship, spectacle, mythologizing. Surely one continuing difference between television and digital media is the absence of showmen in the Arledge tradition (or, for that matter, in the tradition of any other of television's vaunted programmers and golden guts). In television, the showmen invariably become key power centers and often take over—that's a sure conflict, and obvious disruption, to introduce into a technology company (Net-flix's Reed Hastings is an exception proving the rule).

And sports is money—pure and simple, brute and blatant. The appeal of technology is that you don't need money; you're offering efficiency and innovation, and profound changes in behavior. Sports goes to the highest bidder.

And it's selling. Even to the extent that the overwhelming part of digital media revenues come from advertising, and that the whole business is focused on advertising revenue growth, there is still that *Adbusters* mentality in the digital world. It is one thing to subsist on a vast sea of functionally classified advertising, and even on substantial pieces of digital budgets, but that is much different from the kind of influence and clout and more or less bad manners that you have to put up with to get the deals that make sports profitable. Mark Zuckerberg might not be naturally inclined to grovel and suck, or make excruciating rah-rah small talk before big brand agencies, media buyers, and CMOs the way all network CEOs do when they are pursuing long-term rights deals.

# 24

# TELEVISION AND THE WAY
# WE LIVE NOW

*The Washington Post* in 2007, already under considerable revenue pressure, still made nearly a billion dollars. That same year several senior members of its staff broke away to launch *Politico*, which, in its small-town newspaper approach to covering the federal government—that is, a general tolerance for anything on topic that fit the space (unlimited in the case of the Web)—undercut one of the *Post*'s main franchises. Hence, in some existential sense, the *Post*'s billion-dollar business was converted into an approximately $60 million business (2014).

This new economics of content producers—from AOL and Ya-hoo to *The Huffington Post* and *BuzzFeed*, to the Web sites and app outlets of traditional content makers—has had a logical effect. In-formation and entertainment (i.e., content) had to be cheaper, it had to be more plentiful (i.e., more space and time to fill), and, seeking ever more traffic, it had to appeal to a wider and wider audience.

The methods almost everywhere were aggregation, a modest repurposing of the same material from site to site, user-generated content, a kind of democratized or amateur—and cost free—approach to information and entertainment (similar to one's sister playing the piano for houseguests in the 1920s), and bulk production, from the truly cynical and valueless, to the recruitment of lots of young people to do the best and fastest they possibly could (at the cheapest price), to the goofiest kind of mass sensibility (the cat videos and much other viral pulp), which would become the main drivers of social media.

It was in this that digital media (or all but the most specialized part of it) became the new wasteland.

In a parallel universe, tracking much of the growth of digital, but involving a different economics, talent pool, and sensibility, television was evolving as quickly and as dramatically. As digital media was steadily becoming a lowest common denominator race of traffic, television, entering one of its cyclical golden ages, was becoming a cultural event.

Without anyone's quite being aware, there was a clear juxtaposition, if not competition, between two types of content: the bits and bites and scattershot of digital and the grand narratives and comedic talent of television.

In fact, the sequential real-time availability of these shows, first on DVDs and then in binge-watching streaming form—and then released as first-run complete seasons by Netflix—reaffirmed the narrative structure (the success of *Breaking Bad* is often credited to Netflix binge watching). Without announcement, or much trend analysis, this old media was suddenly as current and influential as new media—in fact, it was one of the central concerns of much social media comment and obsession.

The new television's economic context was not hard to figure out. A paid world demanded sought-after rather than default content. The bill payers in a household made the buying decision for premium channels—and bill payers were older rather than, in the longtime entertainment paradigm, teenagers. And ratings were no longer the only metrics for success. Television had in a sense bifurcated itself between downmarket and upmarket—or between unscripted (that is, reality television) and scripted. Scripted, having had its level raised by premium television, had become a new cultural threshold, speaking to both more segmented audiences and, overall, a more educated media consumer. Another flip had occurred: movies, once a high- as well as lowbrow form, had become a teenage medium; television had become not just adult entertainment, but a high middlebrow form. Digital media became the stuff of short attention spans and restless energy, while television became storytelling on a riveting, epic, moral, how-we-live-now scale: the baby boom trying to understand itself and the world it had wrought.

A moralistic intensity consumes the Internet, lynch mobs pursuing all sorts of political correctness and constant challenges to ideological purity and unrighteous behavior and thought standards and new family values. While television elevates exactly the opposite life view. Its heroes are flawed men and women. Television, once the stronghold of rigid and ritualized behavior, an enforcer, if not inventor, of old family values, an ultimate beacon of hypocrisy, became the land of moral relativism. Among the most successful and culturally significant characters were all manner of men and women at odds with time and place and liberal decorum— and yet, nevertheless, embraced by a liberal audience.

Digital media prosecuted all manner of isms and language and thought deviations, constantly trying to expose the hidden malefactors, while television was celebrating, and profiting from, the expansive view that human nature was complex, perverse, ever secretive, and never what it seemed.

If there was a new television message, it was the reassurance that we were all recognizable, however bent, dark, and unsettled.

If there was a message from digital media, it was that the world was unforgiving, its expectations narrow and unbending, its rough justice bloody.

Once, of course, morality and media were the same, but a reasonable description of much modern media is that it is defined by a divide between morality and entertainment.

What does it suggest that one form of popular media is an enforcer of strict norms, and another seeks to explode them, or at least indulge us in the fantasies of exploding them?

One way of seeing this is in audience terms. A downmarket or, in essence, tabloid audience is always reductive in nature, its message black and white and not shadowed or ambiguous. The upmarket audience, almost invariably a more sought-after and valuable one, seeks a qualitatively different sort of narrative, more unexpected in its outcome, more character driven, and more demanding of its writers' ability to offer an original, and hence more valuable, picture of the world.

## 25

# THE DIGITAL POSTSCRIPT

Those who fail to learn from history are doomed to retweet it.

Nick Denton, the often brutally self-aware founder and CEO of Gawker Media, one of the highest-flying native digital media companies of the last decade, wrote a memo to his staff at the end of 2014 acknowledging that Gawker had faltered in an environment more and more dominated by *BuzzFeed*-type traffic methods.

While Denton also used his memo to try to rally his staff, there was a clear sense of his own weariness. He blamed his fuller personal life, and time away from the office, for Gawker's present problems. And, in an unusual management solution, realizing the limits of his own personal traffic voodoo, he appointed a committee as a more dependable decision-making overseer for the business than he himself to oversee the various parts of Gawker's portfolio.

But, evident in the memo, it was not just that he had changed— the inveterate nightlifer now married and hoping for children—but that the business had changed. At somewhat cross purposes to his desire to better compete with *BuzzFeed* (or admitting that this is impossible), Denton urged his company back to its blogging roots. In this, Gawker becomes one of the constants of digital media: whatever your success has been, you will always be superseded by a next-generation form of the business. *Gawker*, with its digital-generation rancor, superseded, much to many people's horror, *Slate*, Harvard on the Internet, as the state of the digital media art (arguably, digital media appears to have about a five-year life expectancy term limit at the top, give or take).

*Gawker* originally rose to power in a revolution in media efficiency that thought it was a revolution in sensibility. And, indeed, efficiency is quite an extraordinary attraction: faster, cheaper distribution, total word-search capabilities, links to any other material, a general lowering of all intellectual property barriers, speed, access, cost, among other benefits. A parallel, or at least a curious metaphor, is with the revolution in food distribution that began with the Second World War: canned food, frozen food, processed food, fast food. American diets became level and homogenized; flavor, culture, technique became secondary or even irrelevant considerations next to efficiency. Then, later, a rediscovery of sensibility created a counterrevolution and a new, vastly profitable food culture.

The benefits of digital media were, of course, not billed as mere efficiency. The benefits were, rather, little less than a social revolution, involving openness, access, collaboration, participation, a trillion flowers blooming. Instead of the word being delivered from the proverbial hegemonic tree trunk, the word would come from the branches, fed back to the tree, and redistributed accordingly.

But the true medium-message was a much different one. The

real digital advance is, of course, accurate reproducibility—that's the ultimate industrial goal. It's mass production. The unit value drops in terms of both cost of production and its sale price, but greater fortunes are made because much larger scale can be achieved. That's Google and Facebook.

In the beginning it was that the trillion flowers and individualized Web sites would exist in some kind of more level and human equilibrium, with Google providing equal access. But Google and Facebook, thriving on efficiency—and efficiency being what they were good at—imposed a system of regulation and sameness. There was no way to exist in the market except to follow the Google and Facebook rules.

Digital media's efficiency and, to boot, the lack of inventive resistance to it (can you ever truly resist efficiency?), having destroyed traditional media, then began eating itself.

Gawker, however scabrous, actually succeeded in quite traditional media terms. It developed highly branded niche sites with a sales organization able to sell the value of being part of these brands rather than just the value of the numbers of people who visited them. But during the Gawker age, audience thresholds grew from a daunting 10 million monthly visitors as the acknowledged minimum for a high-profile site and big-budget advertising accounts, to a fantastic 50 million visitors as the price of entry, to even an absurd 100 million. Now, in the *BuzzFeed* era (with its claims of 150 million and more monthly visitors), a media company is really a technology company, with its highest resources devoted to automating and increasing the efficiency of audience aggregation. But somewhat confusingly, such automation turns out to require hundreds of people to perform. While Gawker is owned entirely by Denton and has been self-financing for most of its history, *BuzzFeed* has needed vast investment. While Denton has rebuffed all offers to buy his profitable business, *BuzzFeed* searches the market for a greater fool.

Gawker, or the Gawker identity, Denton seemed to acknowledge in his memo, is a casualty in the race for traffic: *Gawker* succeeded because it was a carefully molded product (a small band of young people overseen by Denton—with Denton constantly hiring and firing his editors). But then it morphed into a business with a much larger number of ever-younger people having to produce more and more, and working with less and less editorial vision or leadership. *Gawker* began to focus on an open area of parallel writing (i.e., free writing) designed to enhance its traffic base—but, too, with the natural effect of diluting quality and confusing purpose.

Curiously, or ludicrously, *The New Republic*, the one-hundred-year-old Washington magazine, with a circulation of under fifty thousand, announced at the end of 2014 that it wanted to transform itself into a digital media business. This desire seems to have been born out of a sense that all media is now digital or must be, that, in the conventional wisdom, "digital is the future." Print is the trash heap, and digital is a wide-open world of possibilities and opportunities.

Chris Hughes, the owner of *The New Republic*, made vast sums as a member of the founding Facebook team—as Mark Zuckerberg's fortuitous Harvard roommate, as Hughes is no doubt tired of hearing and a description he would like to overcome. He went out of his way to say *The New Republic* could no longer be a charity case. In this regard, and hardly choosing from the top of the class, he hired Guy Vidra, a former news executive at Yahoo, another company that has been thoroughly outpaced in the medium, and Gabriel Snyder, a former *Gawker* editor (fired, like so many) turned into for-hire digital bureaucrat.

Since 10 million monthly visitors barely signifies in digital media terms, it is hardly far-fetched to estimate that to maintain *The New Republic*'s current level of outsize influence, it will have to transform its 50,000 print readers into 50 million monthly digital visitors. In ballpark terms, the revenue potential for 50 million monthly visitors is $25 million to $50 million a year, at a cost that usually exceeds what you will make on such traffic. (As with Outbrain and other traffic-trading deals, it's a kind of fool's arbitrage.) This is not, of course, an editorial proposition, but the result of better systems management—a hard game, because there are always newer and better systems and systems managers. And, in fact, that is just the digital publishing business now. Undoubtedly it will morph into something even further from publishing as we know it. Denton took advantage of a moment when he could use new technology to bootstrap himself into creating an original and influential new publishing form. But today's "vertically integrated digital media company," in Vidra's self-hoisting words, is another duck altogether.

The peculiar development, full of dramatic irony, is that television, with its more circumscribed audiences making much more active selection and choice, becomes upscale media, and digital, with its mass reach and reflexive actions, becomes the downscale side. Television is a discerning and measured choice, a conscious and affirmative vote, and digital passive—a new sort of half-aware audience of couch potatoes mindlessly shuttled between social media prompts and headlines.

The latter, although often the result of millions of individual contributors, is in essence automated, rote, algorithmic, and, in the end, undifferentiated. The former is, practically speaking, a hand-crafted, elaborate, complex, difficult construction. One a housing development, the other an ambitious piece of architecture.

It is a juxtaposition of two cultures. One creates a system that has value, the other creates individual works that have value. (CBS is not the principal value; its principal value is that it has created and owned things like *NCIS*, a billion-dollar franchise—a key aspect of every entertainment company is the value of its library.)

The former believed it could overtake and replace the latter. But that was a system view—an efficiency model. In the system, you are part of . . . the system. Whereas, making hits is inefficient, making a unique product is an effort to distinguish yourself from the system. Relative conformity versus relative independence. Curiously, the entrepreneurial ethos and romance of the technology world is much more present in the world where a creative product is the currency.

One would be hard-pressed to find, in the great scheme of media executives and chief marketing officers and media buyers, someone who could ably articulate the particular value of an imaginative moment or mood or relationship or leave-taking from everyday life. But that is ultimately what advertisers are buying, that quality of attention and of identification, and what audiences are paying for, a plot worth following, characters worth knowing, a world worth being part of.

In some sense, the future of the future, the higher value of the future, is always analog—handmade, sought after, exclusive (the art market being an extraordinary example). Standardization—digital being the ultimate standardization—occurs and price and value are lowered. Then the culture advances once again toward the unique, the differentiated, the original. Digital's early attraction, its counterpoint to television, was the promise of infinite uniqueness, but the reality, after an era of top-down systemization and control, and the constant optimization of the technology itself, was an effective repetition and blandness—the Hallmark drivel of social media, the qualified and tested lists and headlines of *BuzzFeed*. Meanwhile television, once the land of the banal, became something of a hothouse of the unexpected to which both popular culture and commercial culture (always finely connected) were drawn. In a curious way, twenty-first-century television has become rather closer to the movie culture of the 1930s and '40s that so held the popular imagination that people would go seriously out of pocket for it.

Now the digital industry, wearing out the various novelties of the medium that once propelled its cheap programming, reverts, like cable before it, to its pure distribution function, and seeks out the highest-value products it can provide its customers, which, in the media business, is the extraordinary variety, the quite astonishing inventiveness, and the cultural primacy of television. The revolution that began in the 1950s continues on—leaping over the digital distraction.

# ACKNOWLEDGMENTS

Chip Bayers, my longtime friend and colleague, one of the earliest journalists in the digital world and one of its most discerning observers, has been a critical sounding board for this book. The discussions we have had for many years about the future of the media business continue to bear rich fruit. His views inform every page.

The research firm Schireson Associates has contributed time, resources, and empirical wisdom to this effort. In a world where digital numbers can supply any answers you want, Schireson and various of its principals and partners—Kern Schireson, Ethan Bauman, Jacob Harris, and Nathan Hugenberger—have helped provide rigor and context.

Aspects of this material have appeared in my columns in *USA Today*, *The Hollywood Reporter*, British *GQ*, and *Vanity Fair*. I am grateful to the editors there for their insights and the opportunities they have afforded me.

Adrian Zackheim and Eric Nelson at Portfolio / Penguin have been crucial and valued collaborators. As always, my great thanks to my agent, Andrew Wylie.

*Michael Wolff*
*New York, 2015*

# INDEX